George Hill

Titania's Banquet

Pictures of Woman, and other Poems. Third Edition

George Hill

Titania's Banquet
Pictures of Woman, and other Poems. Third Edition

ISBN/EAN: 9783744711159

Printed in Europe, USA, Canada, Australia, Japan

Cover: Foto ©Thomas Meinert / pixelio.de

More available books at **www.hansebooks.com**

TITANIA'S BANQUET,

PICTURES OF WOMAN,

AND

OTHER POEMS.

BY

GEORGE HILL.

THIRD EDITION, REVISED AND ENLARGED.

NEW YORK:
D. APPLETON & COMPANY,
90, 92 & 94 GRAND STREET.
1870.

PREFACE.

THE first edition was published anonymously, and with contents so limited, and to some extent otherwise different from those of the next (entitled " The Ruins of Athens, Titania's Banquet, a Mask, and other Poems "), that the author concluded, though, as he now thinks, injudiciously, not to style the latter a second. *In it, however, was mentioned the appearance of the former.* In consequence of numerous additions and various other modifications, the present edition differs materially from both.

The titles of some of the pieces considered, it perhaps may appear needless for him to remark that they were suggested by either objects or incidents observed by him while absent from the United States.

CONTENTS.

	PAGE.
TITANIA'S BANQUET,	9
PICTURES OF WOMAN:	
1. The Spanish Mountain-girl,	32
2. Leila,	35
3. Mary,	36
4. Genevieve,	37
5. In Memoriam,	38
6. The Portrait,	40
7. Ruth,	42
8. Lavinia,	43
9. The Unnamed,	45
10. A Health to Agnes,	47
11. Sue,	48
12. To the Subject of a Portrait,	49
13. Night-piece to Helen,	50
14. Gertrude,	51
15. To Edith, silent,	52
16. Eugenia,	52
17. Marion,	53
18. Anacreontica Casta,	54
19. The Cavalier's Serenade,	55
THE RUINS OF ATHENS,	56
The Maiden's Song to the Violets,	71
To a Flower found among Ruins,	73

CONTENTS.

	PAGE
The Lost Pleiad,	75
To a Migrating Sea-bird,	77
To Sweet-brier Blossoms,	79
To an Ancient Gold Coin,	80
Lament of the Emigrating Indian,	84
To a Flower from the Athenian Acropolis,	86
Evening at Sea,	88
Love and Reason,	90
The Glen and the Burial,	93
To Young Wood-roses,	96

SONNETS:

1. May, 97
2. To a Young Mother, 98
3. Twilight at Sea, off Delos, 98
4. Crossing the Beach of Aboukir Bay, 99
5. Napoleon, 100
6. Recollections of Greece, 101
7. Absence, 101
8. To the Author of the "Life of Ashmun," 102
9. To the Painter of the Panorama of Quebec, 103
10. Scio, 103
11. Love of Spiritual Beauty, 104
12. The Grave of Fitz-Greene Halleck, 105
13. Scene revisited after the Death of a Friend. 106

Early Spring,	107
The Mariner's Farewell,	108
Autumn in Greece,	109
Song of the Grecian Youth,	111
Cape Colonna,	112
To a Withered Rose from the Banks of the Meles,	114
The Self-exiled's Farewell,	116
The Self-exiled's Return,	118
IDLINGS WITH NATURE,	120
Battle of San Jacinto,	136
Poetry of the Woods,	138

CONTENTS.

	PAGE
The Fall of the Oak,	140
Ruins of the Temple of Jupiter Panhellenius,	143
Life,	145

PIECES OF A RELIGIOUS CHARACTER:

1. The Two Worlds,	147
2. The Past and the Present,	148
3. The Nuns' Evening-Hymn,	149
4. Ægean Vespers,	150
5. The Death of St. Clara,	151
6. To the Infant Saviour,	152
7. The Penance of St. Mary,	154
8. Penitence,	155
9. Matins,	156
10. Life beyond the Grave,	157

Circe and Telemachus,	158
The Artist's Grave,	161

DEFINITIONS:

The Time-server,	162
The Pulpit Quack,	162

The Revel,	163
Song,	164
Vision of June,	165
To a Nun heard singing,	166
To a Picture,	167
Leaders of the American Revolution,	167
Relics of Nobility,	168
To a White Lily,	168
Written in an Album,	169
Mitylene,	170
Version of a Greek Relic,	170
Epistle to a Belle,	171
Scotch Epistle,	174

TITANIA'S BANQUET.

SCENE.—*An open Plot in a Forest.*

Enter two Fairies.

Song.

FIRST FAIRY.

OH, come to my bower,
    At the noontide hour,
And wait not for the moon !
Oh, come where the wood-flowers drip and twine !
We have bees for pipers, dew for wine ;
    Oh, come ! for the rose fades soon.

SECOND FAIRY.

Said the Fairy-knight,
    I am a Sprite
Of the free and sunny air ;
I may not be your love, and dwell
Where the pale flowers weep, and the cold founts well,
    And your bower, where the owls hoot, share.

I am a lover of the light, and like
Not these your shadowy, unfrequented haunts,
These leafy cloisters, whose pale nun, the shy
Cold wood-rose, ever weeps in her dank cell.
The owl no more winks at a sunbeam here
Than at a star at midnight. List! what stirs?

FIRST FAIRY.

The toad slinks to her covert, and the gnat
Gives o'er his hum. Some charm's abroad.

SECOND FAIRY.

If so,
Titania comes; these hushed portents are still
Her harbingers.

FIRST FAIRY.

Yon star that but now winked
In the horizon, like a glowworm on
Some low, moist bank—look! where it mounts and
burns
Bright o'er our heads.

SECOND FAIRY.

It is her torch-bearer.

TITANIA *and her Train approach.*

FIRST FAIRY.

A motley troop!

SECOND FAIRY.

A motley! one would think
She'd, of their henchmen, robbed the courts of all
The shadowy kings 'twixt here and Mariban.
There's one that wears a feather in his cap
Plucked from the gray hood of a Lapland owl—
Look! with a snow-flake on it. The bright shell,
Wherewith yon dwarf elf bonnets his swart brow,
Is from a shoal of Muscat; and the robe,
Spangled with gold, and strung with small white pearls,
The Spirit of the brown and buskined leg
Trails at his sun-burnt knee, was once the ear
Of a small mouse that burrows in an isle
Where their gold apples watched the Hesperides.

FIRST FAIRY.

What holds she by a silken twine? a beetle?

SECOND FAIRY.

An Ethiop sent him from the reeds of Nile
To be her trumpeter. His spots of green
And gold her fancy won. The dolt! there's no
More music in his horn than in the scream
Of Scylla's seamews. Yet he swears he has
Heard a star sing, and into silence charmed
The chords of Memnon; nay, unsphered the moon,
Mistaking his dull drone for the sad harp

Of her Endymion.   The knave! he'll thrive
At court.

FIRST FAIRY.

Ay; should he not, he were no knave.

Flourish.   Enter TITANIA *and her Train.*

TITANIA.

A weary march we've had; now rest.

Enter PUCK.

TITANIA.

Whence come
You, Puck?

PUCK.

From where 'tis noon when here 'tis midnight.

TITANIA.

Met you with Oberon?

PUCK.

No, Queen! nor did
I chance to hear of him: but, if you'll send
A messenger to Ormus, to the girl,
The Arab fisherman's daughter, her who sits
By the sea-bank, and, like a mermaid, sings,
Braiding her dark locks with small, golden coins,
Stamped with strange legends and the images

And superscriptions of old Eastern kings,
Belike you'll find him sleeping in her lap.

FAIRY. [*Aside.*]

Pale as the snow-drop at her foot! Now will
She pinch this Ismael siren into more
Colors than spot an Indian shell.

TITANIA.
       What elf
To-night has seen him? Speak! Will none obey?

FAIRY.

Within a green plot of the wood,
An aged, withered oak there stood,
Like a hermit, gray and lone,
Breathing forth his orison,
Or a wizard, near the centre
Of whose dread round no Sprite may venture,
A withered leaf was, here and there,
Heard, at times, to twirl in air,
All beside was still and bare;
Rank the grass beyond it grew,
On each blade a drop of dew,
But where, in the cold moon's ray,
Dim and jagged its shadow lay,
Grass nor grew, nor dew was sprinkled,
Sprite nor tripped, nor glowworm twinkled;

There saw I the Elfin King
Sleeping in a fairy ring.

TITANIA.

There let him sleep.—What Spirit have we here?
An Ethiop? He has the brow of one.

PUCK.

Your majesty! I found him in a grot
By the Dead Sea. I questioned him of whence
And what he was; whereat he shook his head,
And, with his sooty finger, pressed his lip.
He makes no answer, but points to the shore;
Arrived at which, I heard a low strange voice,
As of a sea-nymph singing in her cave,
And looking down, a thousand feet below
The water's unmoved surface, roofs discovered,
Columns, and battlements, and pavements, strown
With gems, and gold, and sea-weeds, intermixed,
Lit up by subterranean fires, and lamps
Of subtile naphtha; sitting by which, a Sprite,
In likeness of a Nereid, from a book
Chanted strange symbols. I had heard the tale
Of Sodom and Gomorrah, now the haunts
Of powers, 'tis said, that sway the elements
Of fire and water, so, surmised that she
Muttered some charm of virtue to withhold
Their submarine dominions from the grasp
Of hostile demons, who might else invade

Them for their riches. With a pearl, I found
Loosed from a shell of the Arabian Sea,
I won this Fairy, as I deem he is,
To join my troop; not doubting but he might
Be tempted, by the pleasures of our court,
To exchange for them the sullen life he led
In sultry waters and the oozy halls
Of sunken cities, and, in time, disclose
The secret of the charm that guards their treasures.
They call him Asphalt. More of him I know not.

TITANIA.

Is your troop ready?

PUCK.

They are sleeping, Queen.
Black and white elves, brown and gray,
You are summoned; elves, obey!
Come from crevice, nook, and hole,
Lily-cup, and cell of mole,
Bower, and bank of moss-turf green,
At the bidding of your Queen.

Enter Troop.

TITANIA.

Fairies, know that we do expect, to-night,
To grace our revelry, a puissant Spirit,
Who sways the sceptre of an Orient king,
One of the famed enchanters that, of old,

Where the Chaldean reed now rustles, saw
Their proud seats pinnacled amid the clouds.
Him, as it chanced, with all his palaces,
An earthquake swallowed, long before the flood.
Thus sepulchred, his seat of empire is,
Fathoms below the deep sea-bed, possessed
By this same Spirit, or, as he is styled,
Prince of the Gnomes, the swart elves, whose haunts are
The unhewn chambers of the rock, the deep
And sunless caverns. Him I would receive
With all due form, seeing he doubtless deems
Us, who these wild and wooded walks frequent,
Strangers to the imperial pomp, the gold,
The gems, and syrups, that endow the East.
Therefore, mark well my bidding, nor alone
Mark, but see done, with speed that shall outstrip
The meteor's glance, no sooner seen than o'er.

FIRST FAIRY.

The solid earth to us is as a shadow.

SECOND FAIRY.

We'll dart through as sunbeams do through air.

TITANIA.

I would have all things rare and delicate:
Wines in old jars, stamped with the seals of kings

Whose sepulchres were dust long ere the Sophi
Revelled in Shushan; liquors in crystal cups,
Whose blush would shame the morning's, and whose
    sparkle
Dim the tear she lets fall upon the rose,
The sun-stone, or the pearl that Egypt's Queen
Drank to her paramour.

ASPHALT.

                I know of such,
That have so long been buried in the vaults
Of inhumed cities, they would drink the light
As sands do water—glow like liquid gold.

TITANIA.

Spices I'll have from Ceylon, such as scent
The sea-air for a thousand leagues; incense
Of gums of Afric, sweeter than the lip
Of Cupid, moist with Cytherea's kiss,
Than musk-wood, or Sabæa's odorous fire;
Fruits from all climes within the signs that bound
The sun's march, ripening on their branches, brought
In vases moulded of transparent earth;
Syrups of Hybla, and the bags of bees
That hive the Orient's nectared blush. Away!
                [*Exeunt* PUCK *and his Troop.*

FAIRY.

Shall we have music?

TITANIA.

                Such as shall unsphere
The Pleiades.

FAIRY.

        O Queen! I know a bower
In flowery Thessaly, an odorous shade,
Where the Athenian with the nightingale
In singing strove, and broke her heart. There do
The winged musicians at this hour resort,
Startling the midnight silence, till each leaf
Seems a melodious tongue. Thither will I,
And so bewitch them with a song I heard
A star sing to a mermaid, as she lay,
Her white arm floating, like a moonbeam, on
The still sea-wave, that they shall hither flock,
Like halcyons, to a sea-nymph's wreathèd shell.
                           [*Exit, singing.*

Song.

    My couch is not where the wood-flowers drip
      In the noontide shade; but I lie,
        When day is done,
        Where a curtain's spun
      Of the mist of the sunset sky.
        The moon's cold ray
        Is not my day,

But I wake, as fades the star,
  The winking light,
  That follows the night
O'er the green sea-isles afar.

TITANIA.

My subtle minister, you've power to shape
The elements?

ASPHALT.

I have; what would the Queen?

TITANIA.

Rear me a palace straight, whose pride shall shame
All we have heard of Babylonian bowers,
Of Memphian columns, and the pictured roofs
Of Mongol capitals; wherein to dwell,
The gods (if such there be) would gladly quit
Their famed Olympus.

ASPHALT.

To hear is to obey.
[*Palace rises to the sound of subterranean music.*

FAIRY.

Oh, glorious! The airy vault of heaven,
Sprinkled at midnight with ten thousand stars,

Is not more lustrous than this lamplit dome;
The columns seem of gold and ivory,
The capitals of sparkling stones, that show
Like tops of clouds at sunset.

TITANIA.

Glorious!
What trump is that?

ASPHALT.

The Prince's. I should know
His flourish, since full many a time it has
At midnight summoned me. 'Tis of a shell
That once was blown before the argosy
Of a sea-king of Oman.

FAIRY.

Look! this way
He comes, preceded by a sooty troop,
Whose pennons, by their lurid torches lit,
Seem shreds of banners, whose dim blazonry
Is seen to droop where Egypt pyramids
The dust of her old conquerors.

ASPHALT.

Such they are;
Woven of threads of Ophir gold by maids,
Whose mummies were uncatacombed and sold

For incense, long ere stricken by the sun,
The stony lyre of Theban Memnon[1] rang.

FAIRY.

A swart troop, truly! but sparkling with gems,
As they had robbed the Orient, or shaken
The powdered gold from Berenice's hair.[2]

Flourish. Enter the PRINCE *and his Train.*

TITANIA.

Welcome to Fairy-land! You see not here
The wealth and pomp of Orient courts; and yet,
To excuse our entertainment, were to seem
To task your courtesy. Your wish is ours.

PRINCE.

Thanks, gentle Queen! This palace were a home
For proud Semiramis. True it is that we
Inherit the once gorgeous halls of kings,
Where throned they sat, each like a sun beneath
The glorious awning of an evening cloud;
But they are such no more. The imagery,
On the stained roofs of their long-buried domes,
Is dim with subterranean damps, and lit—
As graves by tomb-lamps—by the dull, cold rays
Of lurid torches by nepenthe fed;

---

[1] Statue of Memnon, said to sound when so stricken.
[2] The constellation of that name.

And all the rich embroidery, wherewith
Their walls were decked, is now but hanging shreds,
The air that's moved but by an insect's wing,
Would shake to dust. The carvèd flowers, that wreathed
Their lofty capitals, are cropped by time;
And mouldered bones the pavement strew, which once
The looms of Persia did conspire to deck
In colors richer than the scarf of Iris.
Their wines, their goblets, gems, and gold, are ours;
But seldom do we breathe the upper air,
And gaze upon the vault beneath whose light
You nightly hold your sprightly revels.

Enter MESSENGER.

MESSENGER.

Queen, we've done your bidding well,
Caught the dew-drop as it fell,
Cold and pure as maiden's eye,
From the summer sunset sky.
Syrups of the Orient
In king-cups[1] we here present;
Flowers, untasted by the bee,
'Tis a feast to smell and see;
Violets, as nun's eye meek;
Roses, shamefaced as her cheek;

[1] The flowers so called.

Cloying, till lovesick to death,
The musk zephyr with their breath,
Sweeter than Aurora's, sent
From her Indian spice-wood tent;
Lilies, whiter than e'er set
Dian in her coronet;
Snow-drops, you would say are snow;
Berries of the mistletoe;
Cherries, like to maiden's lips;
Comfits of the tropic; drips
Not from old Hymettus, honey
Sweeter than we bring thee; sunny
Gums we have, that, if fired, shall
With fragrance so your sense inthrall,
You'll think yourself, nay, wish to be,
Evermore an odorous tree;
Emmet's eyes, as small and bright
As diamond-dust; with mushrooms, light
As froth of milk, or thistle-top;
Nuts, sweet as pines of Tempe, drop;
Thigh of home-bound bee, so yellow,
Ne'er was gold that was its fellow;
Ants, seethed as red in fountain hot
As e'er was crab in huswife's pot;
Grapes, through which the sun, see! passes,
As they were wine in crystal glasses;
Water from the spring,[1] we're told,
Makes a young maid of an old,

[1] Fons Juventutis.

That if, with chaste lip, you drink it,
Poured by Hebe you will think it,
From beakers she has kissed, that never
Lose their spicery, sweet forever.
But, why further tell how, sought
Through air, earth, and sea, we've brought
All that's sweet to eye, smell, taste,
To deck out your fairy feast?
Stars are winking, time fast flies;
Strike up, minstrels! Tables, rise!

[*They rise to the sound of subterranean music, with* Spirits, *like* Wood-nymphs, *as Attendants.*

PRINCE.

Sure Orpheus plays, and, at his bidding, comes,
Unseated from the Stygian shore, Elysium!

FIRST FAIRY.

The wine that sparkles in yon crystal cup
Is liquid ruby!

SECOND FAIRY.

Its foam liquid pearl!

THIRD FAIRY.

I'd pawn my immortality for but
Three drops of such nectareous brightness. Pray,
What mole unearthed it?

ASPHALT.

                          One whose burrow is
The sods of Babylon. 'Tis from a jar
Stamped with the seal of Queen Semiramis—
A dove bearing a dagger in its beak:
A bright and drowsy liquor, of which she
Would make her lovers drink, and, when they dreamed
Their souls were revelling in Elysium, slew them.

As the Banquet proceeds, enter PUCK *and* OBERON, *invisible to the Banqueters.*

OBERON. [*To* PUCK.]

You see this flower. I plucked it from the root
Of a Cimmerian hemlock. It was ne'er
Touched by a sunbeam; the cold drops that slake
Its speckled cup fell, in the moon's eclipse,
From a dead leaf of nightshade. Mark you?

PUCK.

                                              Ay.

OBERON.

Take it, and, when their mirth is highest, shake
The dew from it into the charmèd air,
And, like a dream from the vexed sleeper's eye
Woke by a thunder-clap, these conjured shapes
Of pillars, goblets, and attendant nymphs,
Will, in an instant, vanish into nothing.

PUCK.

Your Majesty! the ripple is not spent
That wet my buskin, as but now I trod
The Red Sea shallows; and full oft, to-night,
I've done your biddings in the farthest Ind.
I'm hungrier than a sea-frith at low ebb,
And thirstier than its sands, and much more prize
A drop of the bright liquor which I see,
At your Queen's lip, her merry eye out-sparkle,
Than all the gems of Pegu, though each were
A diamond, and that an Alp.   Oh, no!
I'm in rare mood to help you make a feast,
But not to mar one.

OBERON.

Go!   One service more,
And then we'll rob the bee of sweets she hives
From the Arabian rose, or, if you will,
Sup with the Orient on spicèd dew,
And feel her odorous sigh fan us to sleep.

[*Exit* PUCK, *singing.*

Song.

Said the Fairy-knight,
The will-o'-wisp light
Fast flies, I wearily follow;
Oh! where shall I sleep, my love?   Oh! where?
The dew falls chill, and mirk is the air,
As I roam o'er hill and hollow.

Said his love, I've a bower,
Where, at midnight hour,
The wood-crickets merrily sing;
And thine it shall be,
When you win for me
The gold on the beetle-fly's wing.

PRINCE.

Methought I heard strange music in the air.

TITANIA.

'Twas but the sighing of some passing breeze.
[After a brief interval, PUCK does as he was bidden, and, amid electric flashes and intonations, the scene vanishes.

OBERON.

Ha! bravely done!

[Exit.

PRINCE.

What mockery is this?

TITANIA.

Some trick, I trow, of Puck and Oberon.
Be not surprised!

PRINCE.

I do but smile, yet trust
Your lord's not often in these humors.

TITANIA.

Oh!
Often, but ever, since the Arabian girl

Enticed him with her spells to leave our troop
And green-wood haunts, for sultry moons, and sands
Whose love-bower weaves the scorchèd beach-shrub;
   where,
With help of herb, ill-boding star, and sign
Of puissant charm, whose powers she knows, they still
Conspire to plague us.   Hence the elements,
She holds obedient to her will, misrule
Wildly confounds: Hyperion's wheels now seem
To fire the solstice, and, anon, to slake
Their burning axle in the icy urn
Of grim Aquarius.   Our summer sleep
We tent with curtains by the musk-rose spun—
Her odorous leaves—not doubting, when we wake,
To hear her bedfellow, the lark, or bee,
As he goes singing to his early work:
But lo! at morn, shaking the hoar-frost from
Her feathery hood, in these, our green-roofed coverts,
Shivers the owl.   The flower that laughs to-day,
As all the year were June, to-morrow weeps
Congealèd drops, and—like the maid whose bridal
Trim was her burial's[1]—in robes she dons
To greet her paramour, the zephyr, dies.
E'en now you see the moon, whose rising seemed
Aurora's, sadly, as if she had failed
To meet Endymion, put out her light,
And go with veilèd face, weeping to bed.

---

[1] See an epigram ascribed to Erinna.

PRINCE.

E'en let her! We have had our revelries,
And, as with mortals, so with fairies, joy
Is still a hurried guest, whose lips, ere we
Can well return their greeting, sigh adieu!
The huntsman's stirring, and the matin-song
Warns the night-goblin to his earthy bed,
And bids the day-star, that anon will thrust
His torch into the morning's chamber, rouse
Her troop of wingèd serenaders. We
Must hence. Away! [*To his train.*]

TITANIA.

To ship! I have a Sprite
Whose song has power to set the ocean flowing,
As 'twere a brook, and loose the hurricane.
[*Flourish. Exeunt omnes.*

Scene changes to the Deck of a Ship under Sail.

Flourish. Enter TITANIA, *the* PRINCE, *and their Trains.*

Song of the Elfin Steersman.

One elf, I trow, is diving now
For the small pearl, and one
The honey-bee, o'er hill and lea
Goes chasing in the sun;
And one, the knave, has pilfered from
The nautilus his boat,
And takes his idle pastime where
The water-lilies float:

And some the mote, for the gold of his coat,
By the light of the will-o'-wisp follow;
And others trip where the wood-crickets pipe
To the owl, in the grassy hollow;
And some, as crows the cock for day,
The fire-fly lights to bed.
Oh, go! my Sprite—late wears the night—
And see them hither sped.

Haste! hither whip them with this end
Of spider's web; oh, haste!
For fairy-time at matin-chime
Must end, 'tis midnight past;
As gallant a crew as the ocean-dew
E'er sprinkled, I'll need ere morn;
Blow, wind, oh, blow! till not a wave
Leap from the deep unshorn.

Blow! till the sea a bubble be,
And toss it to the sky,
Till the sands we tread of the ocean-bed
As the summer-fountain's, dry:
The upper shelves are ours, my elves,
Are ours, and soon the nether
With sea-flowers we shall sprinkled see,
And pearls like dew-drops gather.

Hesperia's[1] lea and green isles we
Have left, and, by the moon,

---

[1] Cape Verde, anciently called *Hesperium*, the plural form of which is here used.

TITANIA'S BANQUET. 31

Seen dark Leone's castled rock,
Like armèd spectre, frown:
And soon we'll seaward leave the star
That lights the southern pole,
And Indian winds feel o'er the deep
Their waves of perfume roll.

More hands! From lake, elves, bower and brake,
Oh haste, ere morn be up;
Our ocean then the brook, I ween,
Our ship the wood-flower cup.
Oh, from the night an hour, ere light,
A long, long hour to borrow!
But crowing cocks are fairy-clocks
That mind us of the morrow.

Ha! hither they come, skimming the foam,
A gallant crew—but, list!
The lark I hear, the day-star cheer,
And see! it lights the mist.
Our work is done, the port is won,
So wind and wave, oh stay!
The matin-bell bids night farewell
And fairy-time. Away!
     [*Flourish. Exeunt omnes.*

PICTURES OF WOMAN.

I.

THE SPANISH MOUNTAIN-GIRL.

Dulces reminiscitur Argos.
Virg.

FROM old Nevada's snowy crest
    The vapors, as they flee,
Melt into air; gone are the showers;
Each bough has now its buds or flowers,
    And every flower its bee.

The birds of June a merry tune
    Pipe to the morn; and, hark!
There comes, bedight in kirtle gay
And broidered snood, a girl whose lay
    Seems borrowed of the lark;

A thing all lightness, life, and glee,
    One of the shapes we seem

To meet in visions of the night,
And, should they greet our waking sight,
   Imagine that we dream;

With glossy ringlet, brow that is
   As falling snow-flake white,
Half-hidden by its jetty braid;
And eye, like dew-drop in the shade,
   At once both dark and bright;

And cheek, whereon the sunny clime
   Its brown tint gently throws—
Gently, as it reluctant were
To leave its print on thing so fair,
   A shadow on a rose.

She stops, looks up, where scents the air,
   A flower of gorgeous dye,
Whose vase, the work of Moorish hands,
A lady sprinkles, as it stands
   Upon a balcony—

Forth leaning from a window high,
   From curtains that half shroud
Her maiden form, with tress of gold,
And brow that mocks their snow-white fold,
   Like Dian from a cloud.

Nor vase nor lady fair she sees,
  Nor gay flower's odorous bloom,
That mountain-girl, but stands with eye
That seems communing with the sky—
  Her visions are of home.

Some lone recess, beyond the line
  Of inland summits wild,
That flower recalls, where, with bright hue
Firing the dell, its fellows grew,
  And she, a happy child.

She sees, beside the mountain-brook,
  Beneath the old cork-tree,
And toppling crag, a vine-thatched shed,
Perched, like the eagle, high o'er head,
  The home of liberty;

The rivulet, the olive-shade,
  The grassy plot, the flock,
The garden, if for use, yet sweet
And gay with tulip, mignonette,
  And shrub that loves the rock;

The gray church-tower, whence called, at eve,
  The bell her thoughts to heaven;
Where, as through pictured lattice dim
The twilight stole, and rose the hymn,
  She wept, and was forgiven.

Mate, sister, mother, may not from
   Her dreaming eye depart,
Nor one—the source of gentler fears,
More dear than all—for whom she wears
   The token at her heart.

Till, see! the rose has left her cheek,
   The gay, bright glance her eye;
Her song has ceased, and motionless
She stands, an image of distress,
   A seeming Niobe.

Go! simple girl, go! whither thou
   That flower wilt once more see
Fire the old rocks, where sparkling well,
Founts that the wild vines shade, and dwell
   The pure, the brave, the free!

II.

LEILA.

WHEN Leila first we meet, perchance
   We little note beside
The timidness, that still betrays
The beauties it would hide;
But one by one they look out from
Her blushes and her eyes,

Like tints from the unfolding rose,
And stars from twilight skies.

And thoughts are hers and words, or grave
Or joyous, ever bent
Each present hour shall be such as
No future needs repent.
In soul or face she shows no trace
Of one from Eden driven,
But, like the rainbow, seems, though born
Of earth, a part of heaven.

III.

MARY.

" Non mille quod absens."

AND thou hast past, with fading flowers
    And falling leaves, away;
Hast set, thou Pleiad, lost to hope,
But not to memory!
Though far and foreign were the clime,
And lone the spot, where thou art laid,
Absence might not thy soul divide
From mine, nor time thine image shade.

A spirit that, though housed within
    A frail and failing form,

Triumphed o'er sorrow, pain, as shines
A star above the storm;
That, as the rainbow spans the cloud,
At summer's sunset close,
As Death his shadows gathered round,
More bright and lofty rose.

With flowers that perish as they bloom[1]
'Twas meet that thou shouldst die,
And gently yield thy soul, as they
Their sweets, without a sigh.
Though early reft of earthly hope,
From earthly trouble free,
The grief is selfish that laments
The loss of one like thee.

IV.

TO GENEVIEVE.

THERE'S beauty in thy cheek and eye,
   Though darkly bright the light they shed,
The beauty imaged by a sky
   Whose sun, not twilight glow, has fled.
Though richest gems thy brow entwine,
   The fairer for each shading tress,
To me they but unheeded shine,
   While gazing on thy loveliness.

[1] Autumn flowers.

That downcast eye, that placid cheek
    So softly fair—the shaded rose—
And low and quiet tones, but speak
    Of gentle passions in repose;
A mind with God and man at peace,
    Like waters, gliding calm, at even,
And blending, in their tranquil face,
    The softer tints of earth and heaven.

v.

IN MEMORIAM.

LADY! till thee I bade farewell,
    I little deemed remembrance o'er
One feeling would regret to dwell
    At parting from my native shore;
But who may on thee gaze, nor feel,
    Feel, with a sigh, the hope were vain,
The wish that time or change should steal
    Thy image from his heart and brain.

Yet not alone with joy we gaze
    On one so innocent and fair;
Pity looks forward to the days
    Of blighted hope or wasting care.
Sure there are those we might regret
    Were born, if not in youth to die;

We would prolong their stay, and yet
  Feel that their home is in the sky.

Lady! I go where roams the bee
  Through bowers that bloom, though summer flies,
And isles are sprinkled o'er the sea,
  Like relics of a Paradise:
But what are scenes, the mind may dress
  Yet Nature fairer paints, to me?
The more they charm, they not the less
  Will but remind my heart of thee;

Will but remind me, with a sigh,
  Of hours so blest, for they were thine,
I half regret that they, since I
  May not recall them, e'er were mine.
Our ship flies fast—a single star
  Shines on her dark and troubled way;
And such thine image, lone and far,
  Along the path of memory.

Oh, still in soul—for time that cheek
  Must shade, that eye dim—ever be
The Psyche Love may elsewhere seek,
  But ne'er shall find if not in thee;
Still make us feel, though long if fled
  Each Eden guest, yet, kindly given,
Some few we have who do but need
  Absence from earth to be of heaven.

VI.

THE PORTRAIT.

"Though lost to life, yet not to memory."
Anon.

PAINTER, my thanks! This form, this face,
   Seem not the work of art;
This melting glance, soft blush, how like
   The picture in my heart!
Too well, alas! as, blending here
   The lights and shades remain,
I feel they want but life, to be
   The lineaments they feign.

For here are eyes as softly blue
   As half-blown violets; hair
The wreath it graces gently binds,
   Yet leaves to sport in air;
And lips, twin-sisters of the rose
   That buds in either cheek,
Seeming as if they more than breathed,
   And, if they would, might speak.

Here's, too, the brow, we'd say that, ere
   Whose fairy arch she drew,
Her softest pencil, Nature chose
   And dipped in twilight dew;
And here the neck, beside which, where
   The shadows shun the light,

The lily were not graceful, nor
Were falling snow-flake white.

Fairer in soul than e'en in face!
With thee how flew the hours,
As all our words were singing birds,
And all our thoughts were flowers!
They were too happy to return;
But who shall wish for me
The power e'en happier to recall,
If e'er, like them, to flee?

Yet to the fading canvas why
The lineaments impart
Of those, though gone, who seem as here?
Still imaged to the heart;
Pictured where still, to memory's eye,
Imperishably dwell
The forms whose mould is not of clay,
The idols of her cell.

Painter! thy tints so well may feign,
That we, perchance, shall seem,
As on each life-like light and shade
We gaze, to more than dream:
The more we miss some part from time
No pencil ever stole;
Those eyes ne'er move, those lips are mute,
And who shall paint the soul!

VII.
RUTH, OR SPIRITUAL BEAUTY.

IN Ruth we feel 'tis not her cheek,
   Though with the rose it vie,
Her eye that shames the violet,
Breath as from Araby;

Tones like to those the dying wind
   Wakes in the lyre,[1] but 'tis
The loveliness, each outward grace
But images, we prize:

The beauty of the soul—a flower
   That ever blooms, survives
Form, feature, nay, not but till they
Have perished, chiefly lives.

Though of the few whose image time
   Sees uneffaced remain,
Of those we sigh to e'er have met,
If ne'er to meet again,

No wild-wood flower, that seeks the shade,
   Unknown but to the bee,
Of summer's mid-day glance more shy,
Than of the world's eye she:

[1] Æolian harp.

A soul whose passions are but as
The rippling wave, which o'er,
The still, pure fount heaven sees reflect
Its image, as before.

VIII.

LAVINIA.

FEW are the dead the living mourn,
And thousands owe to pride
The stone that marks, yet mocks the dust.
Oblivion else would hide;
The loving and the loved like thee,
Pass not unwept away,
But tears their pale, cold relics steep,
As dews the close of day.

The offerings at thy grave should be
Things beautiful, but frail;
Sad tokens—buds, that half-blown die,
And flowers untimely pale;
And dews of summer, soon exhaled,
When brightest ever fleetest,
And broken music, sprightly sounds
Of strains that cease when sweetest.

Thy spirit seemed from some high sphere,
Some sinless Eden, sent,

That Heaven might more reverenced be,
And we more innocent;
Of lighter essence, ever bent
From earthly bonds to spring,
As it had caught the seraphs' fire,
And heard the cherubs sing;

Yet wanting not—though aiming still
At virtues high and rare—
The sympathies that simpler joys
And humbler sorrows share;
Nor sportive fancies, feelings light,
But innocent, nor words
Whose tones express but joyousness,
Like songs of morning birds.

Vain were our hopes, our offerings vain:
The angels would not rest,
Till they, where thou wert wished for long,
Had placed thee with the blest;
Translated, as the starry sign
We nightly see arise,
And shine above the mists of earth,
A virgin[1] of the skies.

It is not that the tribute here
Of humble flowers I twine,

---

[1] The constellation of the Virgin.

Befit, all frail and scentless as
They are, a soul like thine.
Thy virtues need no stone; the heart
Their monument shall be,
Where lies thine image, mourned by love,
And watched by memory.

IX.

THE UNNAMED.

THE time is gone, forever gone,
 Nor mourn I much its flight,
When woman was my song by day,
Nor less my dream by night;
Yet one there is—long be it ere
She grace the choirs above !—
With whom to be perhaps for me
Were still again to love.

Her eye is like a summer eve,
So tranquil, soft its ray,
The window, image of a soul
At peace, or grave, or gay:
And what's her cheek like, but the morn ?
Where still, if one be past,
Appears some new, yet lovelier hue
Perchance than was the last.

Proclaimer of some thought each is,
Some feeling, more intent
On others' wishes than her own,
Nor merely innocent;
Thought, feeling, that, as imaged there,
Oh, more than words may tell,
If woman yet so lovely be,
What was she ere she fell.

When hers we hear, all other tones,
However sweet, seem mute;
To such, of old, 'twere said each Muse
Had lent her voice and lute;
To words that, breathing of the rose
From lips like its young flowers,
The happiness, as well as song,
Recall of Eden hours.

Sought by the world, her presence less
She thinks it needs than prayer,
Her charity a constant guest,
Herself a stranger there;
To flattery bars her ear, but not
To misery her door,
Loves all God loves, but chiefly sees
His image in the poor.

Some heavenly guest, not dweller here,
In soul and face, she seems;

In her the loveliness we see
Of which the poet dreams.
Ah! well, perhaps, that few like her
To our fond gaze are given,
Lest earth should claim, and haply win,
The love we owe to Heaven.

X.

A HEALTH TO AGNES.

BRING me a bright, a stainless shell,
    That murmurs of the ocean-wave,
And fill it with the drops that well
    From some old, haunted fountain-cave!
To her, whose brow would blush to wear
    The Teian wreath, a draught from high!
By earth though treasured, born of air—
    The wine whose Hebe is the sky.

The cup is here and rightly filled,
    That I would drain to love and thee;
And here are flowers, whose dews, distilled
    From skies of summer, soon will flee.
Put by the rose! 'twill ever breathe,
    In fancy, of the Teian bowl;
And crown thee with the lily-wreath!
    'Tis spotless as thy virgin soul.

XI.

SUE.

THOUGH pretty, Sue's nor proud nor vain,
Yet, as the moon, unsteady;
Flighty one'd think her with champagne,
Or like drop slightly heady.

Now in her cheek we see the rose,
Anon, the lily blow;
Mercurius[1] rules the fickle pulse
That bids them come and go.

At one she's seen, in crape, off bidding
Psalms, sermons, at a véndue;
At ten, at ball or circus, flirting,
And merrier than its "Andrew."

This hour she's sighing for some gay
Glib-tongued madcap to tease her;
The next the wight must solemn be
As ghost or ghoul, who'd please her.

Now sprightly, chatty, sparkling like
A beaker of *sal soda*;
Anon, mum, sad, as devotee
Immured in a pagoda.

[1] Planet Mercury.

This week should she some grandee wed
Magnificent as Mago,
The next, for a divorce, we'd see
Her steaming to Chicago.

And sure, if she were helpmate mine,
I doubt I'd so adore her,
On a like errand, rain or shine,
As not be there before her.

XII.

TO THE SUBJECT OF A PORTRAIT.

"Quanto minus est cum reliquis versari quam tui meminisse!"
Shenstone.

GONE! but by love, as imaged here,
 Still seen—a never-setting star
In skies that else were lone and dark,
A sleepless watcher, bright, though far.
No fears disturb, no sorrow dims
Thy spirit's pure and tranquil eye;
Thy sun the light of God's own face,
Thy life one blest eternity.

And as, of orbs that shining note
The needle's course, it heeds but one,
So turn, from eyes that fondest smile,
Our steadfast thoughts to thee alone.

'Twas meet that thou shouldst early die,
Like dews, that linger not till even,
But, having earth refreshed, return,
At morning, to their native heaven.

III.

NIGHT-PIECE TO HELEN.

THE dew-drop sparkles on the tree,
   The moonbeam on the lake,
     The air is stirred
     But where the bird
His night-song trills—awake!
Oh! say not to the rose he sings,
   Or to the lights on high,
But to the flower upon thy cheek,
   The star that's in thine eye!

To cheeks less fair, and eyes less bright
   Leave slumber; up! and bid
     Each star and flower,
     The midnight hour
Unfolds, her beauty hide;
When thine we see, no thought have we
   Of theirs; and who will say,
While thee we hear—how long soe'er
   The night—they wish for day?

XIV.

GERTRUDE.

THOUGH beauty, youth, be hers, not where
    The midnight hour bid flee
The dance, the song, but where the sad,
    The suffering are, is she.
The dying feels, to hear her low,
    Sweet tones, as if forgiven,
Forgets he's here, and seems, in hers,
    To see the smile of heaven.

Not for her own but others' ills
    She mourns, and not the less
Their good, as if but hers alone,
    She makes her happiness:
All for the love of Him—whose love
    She has—the crucified;
Aspiring still like Him to be,
    Both as he lived and died.

Oh, blest! to feel no tie, that binds
    The soul to earth unriven,
And, like the angels, make and have,
    Where'er she moves, a heaven.
This verse to her! for had a soul
    Like hers the tempter met,
This world, perchance, the paradise
    Had been, it once was, yet.

XV.

TO EDITH, SILENT.

SPEAK, lady, speak! nor lest to words
From other lips we'd listen fear!
In them, perchance, we one, in thine
We every Muse may seem to hear.

'Tis not alone the Teian lute
Their tones recall; they ever tell
Of feelings, wishes, calmly pure
As summer sky or fountain-well;

Of thoughts, that, should they linger here,
Yet soon, like morning birds, above
Their wonted flight re-wing, to where
The cherubs sing, and seraphs love.

XVI.

EUGENIA.

HER soul is imaged in her face,
And, as its lights the sky—
Star after star—reveals, so there
Some new-born charm we spy;
Some grace of feeling, or of thought,
In cheek or eye expressed;

And tones are hers like those we hear
If dreaming of the blessed.

Love from all hearts that love she wins,
And ever, in return,
She has a smile for all that smile,
A tear for all that mourn.
Oh! how can she, in soul or face,
Seem one from Eden driven,
On whom, as on a star, we may
Not gaze, nor think of heaven!

XVII.

MARION.

IN others of her sex perchance
  Some single " grace " we see
Here one, another there, adorn;
In Marion meet the "three."

One moulds her feelings, one her thoughts,
And one each outward part:
In her that's nature which the work
Must elsewhere be of art.

Though we some flower the garden yields
To lovelier bloom may train,

To think to more than emulate
The wild wood-rose, were vain.

Ne'er seems she then a thing of earth?
Ne'er wears that brow a frown?
Ne'er till she hears another's worth
Dispraised, or praised her own.

XVIII.

ANACREONTICA CASTA.

TO JULIA.

THE bard of old, if he'd be gay,
"Crown me with myrtle, boy!" would say,
"Bring rose, bring lights, nor let be mute
The soul that slumbers in the lute!"
What need have I of them, to be
As blessed, if not as gay as he?

What need of rose? thy lips' perfume
And cheek have stole its scent and bloom;
What need of lights, so long as I
A star see in thine either eye?
Or why the lute-chord bid resign
The soul of song? that soul is thine.

XIX.

THE CAVALIER'S SERENADE.

In the manner of the Cavalier poets.

UP! bud and bloom,
    The air perfume,
The night-bird nestles nigh;
Nor to the stars, nor rose sings he,
But to thy cheek and eye;
Her breath is sweet, but only till
Thine scents the night, will be,
    And yon bright moon
    Would set full soon,
Did not she wait for thee.

Oh, wake then! Up! and to my suit
A gentle ear incline;
Or speak! and I, unstruck my lute,
Will gently list with mine;
    For who may see
    The darkness flee
From thy bright face, and hear
The music of thy voice, nor think
He listens to a sphere!

THE RUINS OF ATHENS.

ATHENS was visited by the writer at a time when, abandoned by the Greeks, and held by a few Mohammedan troops, it was in the state of all but total ruin and desolation, from which it has since partially recovered. Its present aspect, therefore, except in regard to the ancient remains, may little accord with that exhibited in the following stanzas. Such, combined with other long-continued and like calamitous effects, had been those of the Greek Revolution, that, not only the place itself, with its forsaken, dilapidated dwellings, but the surrounding country, appeared not to have been inhabited for centuries. As in the time of Xerxes, so then they were in the hands of barbarian invaders, and the only Greek we remember to have seen was a captive. The fading foliage, and tranquil, faintly-hazy atmosphere of autumn, harmonized with and served much to heighten the effect of other features of a picture, the impression made by which on the author's mind he must ever despair adequately to describe.

I.

THE watch-fires fade, and, melting into light
  The stars recede in silence till the gun,
Far-flashing, ere the vapors of the night
Have vanished, thunders from the Parthenon.[1]
O'er old Hymettus glows as bright a sun,

[1] Remains of the temple so called.

Odors as fragrant scent the dewy air,
Fields bloom as freshly, streams as sparkling run,
As, gray Athenæ! still the pride were there
Thy time-worn brow has lost, and never more shall wear.

II.

No more the beautiful, but now the lone
Dethronèd queen, all powerless she stands,
Mid shrines dismantled, wall and tower o'erthrown,
Memorials sad of days when her free bands
Wrested from kings their sceptres, and, with hands
Red with the blood of satraps, on her showered
The spoils of conquered gold of subject lands.
The isles their tributary tridents lowered
In homage at her feet; she spake, and nations cowered.

III.

The bark flies on, and shuns the lonely shore,
The bay, whose wave seems never to have borne
A keel, or rippled to the dip of oar:
But the shy sea-bird there has found a lorn
And quiet home, and of the curlew o'er
The hills is heard the melancholy cry;
And where she sat, the peerless, she, before
Whose arms the East bent her imperial eye,
Barbaric bands encamp, their blood-red signals fly.

IV.

The Roman—he, whose eagles should have led,
Like guardian gods, her children to reclaim
The might that slumbers with her glorious dead,
The conqueror and the despoiler—came;
Chained to whose triumph-car, and taught to tame
Her free-born spirit to subjection, she,
Whose sword had been her sceptre, and whose name
A terror to imperial sway, her knee
Bent—when to rise, ah! when, a ruler of the free?

V.

Morn hushed as midnight! save perchance is heard
At times the hum of insect, or the grass
That sighs, or rustles by the lizard stirred:
And still we pause, and may, where empire was
And ruin is, no stone unheeded pass,
No rude memorial, which seems to wear
Vestige of that whose glory, as a glass
Shattered, but still replendent, lives: earth, air,
Whate'er recalls the past, its spirit breathe and share.

VI.

And many a scene, the Muse has pictured true
And time has hallowed, greets the passer-by,
That, wild of shape, or beautiful of hue,
He gladly hails, nor quits without a sigh:

For Nature here has shed o'er earth and sky
Her loveliest tints, and freely strown around
The wonders of her hand. Oh! hither fly!
Thou, who wouldst see variety abound,
Her fairer works invite, her sternly wild astound.

VII.

Ascend! where slopes Hymettus to the plain,
And winds the pathway by the fountain-well:
Though trod no more, though blood the herbage stain,
And by the hearth-stone rusts the shattered shell,
That fired the roof, whose inmates vanquished fell
And left their bones unsepulchred; yet ne'er
The vernal breeze, from Orient bank or dell,
Odors more sweet at morning poured, than there,
From clefts in wild bloom clad, float on the dewy air.

VIII.

The daylight fades o'er old Cyllenè's hill,
And broad and dun the mountain-shadows fall.
The stars are up and sparkling, as if still
Smiling upon their altars:[1] but the tall,
Dark cypress, gently, as a mourner, bends—
Wet with the drops of evening, as with tears—

---

[1] Either to the planets Mars and Jupiter, or to the deities which they represented, or, perhaps, to both, Athenian temples were dedicated, gigantic remains of which, in the latter instance, still remain.

Alike o'er shrine and worshipper,[1] and blends,
More deeply shadowy, with the night, that hears
The owl's lone wail, whose note some lonelier echo
    cheers.

IX.

But high o'er all, lo! towers the Parthenon.[2]
She, like the last of an imperial line,
Has seen her sister structures, one by one,
To time their gods and worshippers resign,
And the stars twinkle through the weeds that twine
Their roofless capitals; and, through the night,
Heard the hoarse drum, and the exploding mine,
The crash of columns, and the shock of fight,
From their dismantled shrines the guardian powers af-
    fright.

X.

Go! thou, from whose forsaken heart are reft
The ties of home, and, where a dwelling-place
Not Jove himself the elements have left,
The grass-grown, undefined arena pace!
Look on its rent, though tower-like, shafts,[3] and hear
The wild winds thunder in their aged face,
Then slowly turn thine eye, where moulders near
A Cæsar's arch,[4] and the blue depth of space
Vaults, like a sepulchre, the wrecks of a past race.

[1] Their ruined temples and dead worshippers.
[2] Remains of the temple of Athenæ on the Acropolis.
[3] Ruins of the temple of Jupiter Olympius.
[4] Triumphal Arch of Hadrian.

XI.

Is it not better with the eremite—
Where the weed rustles o'er his airy cave,[1]
Perched on their summit—through the long, still
    night,
To sit, a watcher by an empire's grave,
—While oft some fragment, sapped by dull decay,
In thunder breaks the silence, and the fowl
Of ruin hoots,—and turn in scorn away
From all pride builds, time levels, till, where prowl
The wolf and bandit, claims her heritage the owl:

XII.

Or, led by Nature, won with Solitude,
Where since creation she has slept on flowers,
Wet with the noonday forest-dew, and wooed
By untamed choristers in unpruned bowers:
Where wells the fountain-stream from rock that
    towers
O'er dells untrodden by the hunter, piled
Ere by its shadow measured were the hours
To human eye,—the rampart of the wild,
Whose banner is the cloud, by carnage undefiled.

XIII.

The song is mute in Epicurus' shade,
And locked in Academe the Muses' well;

---

[1] A hermitage planted on the entablature of these columns.

Sage, sophist, each now moulders, silent laid
Where the weed withers o'er his nameless cell.
Dreamers! but who the darkness shall dispel,
They strove with eye, still baffled, to explore?—
The shadowy bourne, whence who shall come to tell
What life awaits us on that mystic shore
No Delphic voice unveils, no seer's prophetic lore?

XIV.

And never more the voyager shall spy—
Like guardian spirits, watching through the night
His home-bound bark from isle or headland high—
Shrines, whose gray relics strew their mouldered site.
Warned from her home, each old poetic Sprite
Her altar worshipless laments to see;
From lonely dell, or lonelier mountain-height,
The Nymph of fountain, forest-shade, or tree,
As sighs each passing breeze, seems, weeping sent, to flee.

XV.

A hero's dust has vanished where the foam
Breaks o'er the shattered and now tombless stone.[1]
The waves, whose element he loved, here come
To leave but weeds with drifting sea-shells strewn—
A thankless garland; and the wind's low moan,
And sighing grass, and cricket's plaint, there heard,
But faintly breathe, as with reluctant tone,

[1] Supposed sarcophagus of the tomb of Themistocles.

His dirge.   The sands, by human foot unstirred,
The urnless ashes heap, the wave has disinterred.

XVI.

The scorpion lurks, the lizard breeds secure
Where towered the column, reared to him whose
　　name
Had scattered navies, like the whirlwind; sure,
If aught Ambition's fiery wing may tame,
'Tis here; the web the spider weaves, where Fame
Planted her proud but sunken shaft,[1] should be
To it a fetter.   Here no homage claim,
Oh, Glory's favorite! Victory's child! Thy knee,
Thy dripping sword and plume, here vail to Mockery!

XVII.

A small, gray Elf, all sprinkled o'er with dust
Of crumbling catacomb, and mouldering shred
Of banner and embroidered pall, and rust
Of arms, time-eaten monuments, that shed
A cankered gleam on dim escutcheons; where
The groping antiquary pores, to spy—
A what? a name, perchance ne'er graven there;
At whom the urchin, with his mimic eye,
Sits peering through a skull, and laughs continually.

[1] A fallen column, conjectured to have been a part of the tomb.

XVIII.

The pride here sepulchred, the glory mock!
But not the spirit whose old trophies strew,
Like bones of Cyclopean mould, the rock
They pinnacled; though Conquest, where it grew,
Has slaked its ashes with her crimson dew,
And o'er the spot her shadow, Ruin flings,
At Freedom's call it once more wakes. Renew,
Might of old days, your youth! The trumpet rings,
And Battle plumes his shaft, and Victory her wings.

XIX.

The foe retire, but other hordes may band
And build, where Hellas sees the crescent [1] wane,
In each old fastness of her mountain-land,
Rewaste her earth, relink her shattered chain;
But Leuctra, Salamis, Platæa's plain,
And wild Thermopylæ's heroic pass,
The monuments of Nature—these remain.
Perished the stone,[2] but who the sighing grass
Wanders unheeded by where fell Leonidas!

XX.

From cliff and cape the temple, slowly bowed,
May fall, the tomb commingle with the clay

---

[1] Turkish rule.
[2] In the pass a lion of stone was set up in honor of Leonidas.

It rose to shelter, and the mighty shroud
Their memory in deeper gloom, as they
Had never been; her very name decay:
But from the spot, where rose her song in fight,
Her shout, as on the memorable day
She put the armèd Orient to flight,
A spirit breathes, a power, no coming time shall blight.

XXI.

Here stood the Greek, and there the Persian shrank,
Rider on rider thrown, and shield on shield;
Bristling with spears, an iron crop, they sank,
As the ripe harvests to the sickle yield:
Tombless to rot and fertilize the field,
As weeds, they came as conquerors to reap.
Inglorious dust, by mute oblivion sealed,
Satrap and slave, alike forgotten, sleep;
No tongue laments their fall, no tears their ashes steep.

XXII.

Platæa, Marathon! to these, as turns
The plough some warlike relic from its mould,
Shall point the sire; the stripling—as he learns
How the brave band, though nations were enrolled
To swell the Persian's, thinned his host of old—
Shall feel the spark with thrilling memories fraught,
Fire his young breast, the closing ranks behold

Rush fearless on, the weapon grasp in thought,
And follow where they trod, and conquer where they
    fought.

XXIII.

The night wears late, and from her ancient bower
Owl chants to owl her solitary hymn;
The dews are deepening, and the place and hour—
As now the moon her crescent, pale and dim,
Withdraws from heaven, and the meteors shower
On high their vapory and silent light—
Descend with something of a spectral power
    Upon my spirit; for I stand where night,
Ruin, and solitude, speak but of vanished might.

XXIV.

The might of Greece ! whose story, from her birth
A ceaseless epic, ever breathes the lyre—
A song-wave circling to the bounds of earth,
A marvel and a melody; a fire
Unquenched, unquenchable. Castalia's choir
Mourn o'er their altars, worshipless, or gone;
But the free air, their mountain-homes respire,
    Has borne their music onward, with a tone
Shaking earth's tyrant race through every distant zone.

XXV.

The weary spirit, that forsaken plods
The world's wide wilderness, a home may find

Here, where the dwellings of long-banished gods,
And roofs long tenantless, to dust consigned,
Untomb the thoughts no spell has power to bind—
The loved, but lost, whose soul's life is in ours,
As incense in sepulchral urns enshrined,
The sense of blighted or of wasted powers,
The hopes whose promised fruits have perished with
    their flowers.

XXVI.

Approach! but not thou favored one, thou light
And sportive insect, basking in the ray
Of youth and pleasure, heedless of the night.
Dreamer! the shapes that in thy pathway play,
Thy morning pathway, elsewhere chase! Away!
Come not, till, like the fading weeds that twine
Yon time-worn capital, the thoughts that prey
On hopes of high but baffled aim, decline,
And, weary of the race, the goal unwon resign.

XXVII.

Is thy hearth desolate, or trod by feet
Whose unfamiliar steps recall no sound
Of such as, in thine early days, to greet
Thy coming hastened? Are the ties that bound
Thy heart's hopes severed? Hast thou seen the ground
Close o'er her, thy young love, and felt for thee
That earth contained no other? Look around!
Here thou mayst find companions; hither flee!
Where glory, empire were, but long have ceased to be.

XXVIII.

Temple and tower, lo ! crushed and heaped in one
Wide tomb, that echoes to the Tartar's cry
And drum, heard rolling from the Parthenon,
The wild winds sweeping it, the owl's gray eye
Gleaming among its ruins, and the sigh
Of the long grass that unmolested waves.
Oh, ye, whose proud old monuments are by,
Arise ! one effort more ! E'en recreants, slaves,
The very stones should arm, heaped on heroic graves.

XXIX.

But so it is : Earth from her old lap shakes
Cities as dust; the myriads to-day,
If not to happiness, to hope awakes,
To-morrow fertilize their kindred clay.
The admired of nations, she, who scorned decay
And laughed at time, lo ! where she nightly hears
Barbaric foes their armèd watch array,
Mid temples prostrate, weeds whose dewy tears
O'er roofless homes are wept, no friendly taper cheers.

XXX.

Here let me pause, and blend me with the things
That were, the shadowy world, that lives no more
But in the heart's cherished imaginings,
The mighty and the beautiful of yore :

It may not be; the mount, the plain, the shore,
Whisper no living murmur, voice, or tread,
But the low rustling of the leaves, and roar
Of the dull, ceaseless surf, and the stars shed
Their light upon the flower whose beauty mocks the dead.

XXXI.

Day dawns; and many a mountain known to song
Lifts her old altar, hymned by bird and bee,
As wheeling soars the eagle from among
Their dim, blue peaks, in lone sublimity:
Its incense is the breath of shrubbery,
Its smoke the clouds, as, borne from each high place
Whose gods[1] have vanished, they dissolving flee.
Nature resumes her worship, and her face
Unveils to Him whose shrine and dwelling are all space.[2]

XXXII.

Farewell to Greece! The ship bounds on her way,
Freshens the breeze, and soon is seen no more,
As fast and far the lessening isles decay,
And headlands sink, Athenæ's lonely shore.
Apart her chief the white deck paces o'er,

---

[1] Pagan deities formerly worshipped there.
[2] "Whose temple is all space."—*Pope*.

And greets with stern delight his wingèd home:
Heedless is he how wind or wave may roar,
Nor knows a joy, let wreck or battle come,
Like that which now he feels o'er the blue deep to roam.

THE MAIDEN'S SONG TO THE VIOLETS.

FAIR flowerets ! ye are laughing now,
　　Born for a little while,
So short-lived and of footstep shy,
Had mine not hither strayed, no eye
　　Had seen you bloom and smile.
I joy to meet you in my walk,
　　So daintily arrayed,
And yet 'tis not without a sigh,
　　To think how soon you fade,
　　Frail infants of the Spring !
　　　　That play
　　In her green lap awhile,
　　　　Then pass away.

It were some comfort, might ye know
　　Ye are so fresh and fair,
That now unseen, unscented blow,
　　Save by the sun and air,

Or one like me, who, chance-led, here
Surprised you, nurslings of the year!
    Here live, here die!
Ye bloom not for the world's cold eye,
   So heedless of the poem, we
   Still spoken hear, or written see
By Nature, it cares not to look
On e'en the pictures of her book,
    And such are ye.

Laugh while you may! ere night, I fear
   Your blossoms will be shed;
'Twill grieve me, in my early walk,
   To come and find you dead.
By this green bank, in this lone shade,
So long I've watched you, flowers, so long,
   At morning and the even-song,[1]
    Ye in my path have played,
Like younger sisters, that I feel
A sadness o'er my spirit steal
At parting, and could almost pray
We might together pass away.

[1] Vespers.

TO A FLOWER FOUND AMONG RUINS.

WHAT dost thou here, thou lovely flower?
    The beautiful and brave
Are silent now in this lone tower;
    Go! wither o'er their grave!
Wall-rent and moss-grown turrets moan,
    And weed-clad arches sigh;
For thee too sadly deep the tone
    That speaks of times gone by.

Go, where the rose, the myrtle, blow!
    These halls are not for mirth;
The echoes my lone footfall now
    Awakes, seem not of earth.
The voice of song has with the wind
    Of other times passed on,
And thou art left to bloom behind
    In loveliness alone.

So from the past, the waste of thought
    And feeling, haply springs

Some hope—how dark, alas, if not!—
  To which the future clings;
A flower that blooms where else but blight
  And desolation dwell,
A star that sets not, though the night
  Its beam may not dispel.

THE LOST PLEIAD.

Sterope, one of the Pleiades, or Seven Stars, is said to have at a remote period disappeared, having, according to mythology, been enamoured of a mortal.[1]

THERE were seven sisters, and each wore
   A starry crown, as, hand in hand,
By Hesper woke they led the hours,
The minstrels of his virgin band.

And Love would come at eve, as they
Were met their vesper hymn to sing,
And linger till it ceased, with eye
Of raptured gaze and folded wing.

For ne'er on earth, in air, were heard
More thrilling tones than, to the lyre [2]
Of heaven timed, rose from the lips,
The chords of that young virgin choir.

But they were coy, or seeming coy,
Those minstrels of the twilight hour,

[1] Smith's Class. Dic.
[2] The constellation so named, here supposed to intone what is termed "the music of the spheres."

Nuns of the sky, as cold and shy
As blossoms of the woodland bower.

'Twas eve, and Hesper came to wake
His starry troop, but wept; for one,
The brightest, fairest of the group
Where all were bright and fair, was gone.

They found, within her bower, the harp
To which was tuned her vesper hymn,
The star-gems of her coronet,
And one was with a tear-drop dim.

They told how Love had lingered till
The twilight's earliest watch was o'er;
But he was gone, and she, the mourned,
The lost one, seen in heaven no more.

TO A MIGRATING SEA-BIRD.

THE wave still ripples to the shore,
　　Woke by thy parting wing;
Yet, high, where glows the twilight o'er
　　Thy path, I see thee spring.
The airy goal is won, at last,
Whence the sure path, by instinct traced,
　　Notes thy unerring eye,
To lake, or pool of reedy moor,
Where, haply, thou hast built before,
　　And heard thy ducklings cry.

There choose thy mate, thy nursery weave,
　　Nor hawk nor man molest
Thy quiet brood, till on some eve
　　Like this, they quit their nest;
By Cola's wild, unpruned recess,
That, to the hunter, bars ingress,
　　And suns of sultry beam;
Or, where the water-lily sleeps,
Rustles the reed, the alder weeps,
　　By Lena's lake and stream.

Lone bird! a happy lot hast thou,
An empire kings might envy! now,
    Where icy storm-winds rock
Thy willowy cabin, lodged, anon
Diving where pools of Amazon
    The tropic umbrage mock.

Birds have their cares as well as men;
Yet, it may be, thy simple ken
    Notes but the passing one;
The future, past, alike unspied,
All memory would vainly hide,
    And fear as vainly shun.

The graves, beneath thy roving wing,
Of former mate or nursling, bring
    No tear into thine eye;
But thy affections still obey
A kindlier law, unwept decay,
    And unregretted die.

TO SWEET-BRIER BLOSSOMS.

FAIR nuns ! sequestered by the woodland spring,
  Where haply few will see you bloom, or die,
No passing breeze your morning offering,
  Your dewy sweets, forsakes but with a sigh.

Proudly yon shrubs their scentless buds unfold,
  You, meekly blushing, timidly expand,
Blooming as Hebe's cheek, yet chastely cold
  As moonlight lilies cropped by Dian's hand.

O'er such in Tempe-vale, and where they scent
  The dews of Araby, the zephyr sighs ;
Such Eve, as weeping from its bowers she went,
  Plucked as memorials of Paradise.

TO AN ANCIENT GOLD COIN FOUND ON THE PLAINS OF TROY.

> "Thou com'st in such a questionable shape
> That I will speak to thee."
>
> Hamlet.

A COIN we call thee, but thy name and date
    Defy, I ween, all probable conjecture;
Perhaps, when Troy was in her palmy state,
    Struck to commemorate some feat of Hector;
Perhaps, coeval with the days of Jubal,
Cast by that Cain whose luckier name was Tubal.[1]

Time-eaten relic! within whose dim round
    The memories of bygone ages dwell,
Like shapes sepulchral, disinhumed and bound
    Within the magic ring by wizard spell;
Thou cabinet of shadowy portraits, glass
Wherein the phantoms of dead empires pass!

Rome, Carthage, Tyre, those war-ships on the tide
    Of time, are now as they had never been:

---

[1] "Tubal Cain ... an artificer in every work of brass and iron."—*Gen.* iv. 22.

Their battle-ensigns, that had earth defied,
   Ages ago were struck, and piecemeal seen
Into its dark Lethean waves to drop,
While thou, a bubble, floatest at their top.

Thy fellow-bubbles—Cæsars, Caliphs, Sophis,
   Kings, Consuls, Tribunes, Moguls, Magi, Sages—
All who have left to dust their bones and trophies,
   And names (where not misspelt) to after-ages—
The lions, *ne plus ultras*, of their day,
The marvels, Trismegisti, where are they?

Where Thoth, where Cheops, Ninus, Babel's founder,
   And he, who saw himself, with much amaze—
Of his own dream the practical expounder—
   Hurled from his throne, and, oxlike, sent to graze!
Where many more of old and modern story,
Jew, Gentile, Greek, Barbarian, Whig, and Tory!

Where was thy birthplace, thy primeval bed?
   Did Kaff infold thee in his rocky vest?
Or wast thou shaken by the thunder's tread
   From Gebeltar,[1] or Himalaya's crest?
Tried in some now extinct volcano's fire?
Or, brought from Ophir in a ship of Tyre?

Were thy device and legend visible,
   In that dilapidated face some mark

---

[1] The ancient name of Gibraltar.—See Bryant's Mythology.

Haply the hierologist might spell,
   Of ages styled, ere Belus reigned, " The Dark ; "
Some mystic type, perchance the monogram
Of some old Sheik anterior to Ham.

What transformations hast thou undergone?
   Yet still—whate'er thy feature, form—caressed :
How oft been cheaply lost, or dearly won?
   Yet still, wherever met, a welcome guest :
For doubtless thou hast travelled long and far,
Ere rags were cashed, or promises at par.

Thou mayst, when Ilium was destroyed by fire,
   Have melted from the ear of some rich beauty,
Or, as a chord to love-lorn Sappho's lyre,
   Or royal Nimrod's hunting-bow, done duty,
Or, brought at Aaron's bidding, helped to mould
The statue of a god—the calf of gold.

Thou mayst with Cadmus into Greece have come,
   Or been a link in Cecrops' coat-of-mail ;
Ulysses may have filched thee from his chum,
   Or Homer pawned thee for a pot of ale,
Whose epic rhapsody too much of slaughter
Breathes, to have been a nursling of cold water.

Or was Troy but—as some may deem proved fully—
   A dream? the tumulus before my eye,

Not heaped o'er Ajax,[1] but some other bully?
  Helen's abduction, an egregious lie?
The Iliad's hero, a fictitious person?
  In short, the author a mere Greek Macpherson?

What though old Priam's battle-trump no more
  Rings, but the Turk, at Agamemnon's post,
Or where Pelides greatly sulked and swore,
  Recumbent nods in opiate visions lost,
I scorn the pedant and his prosing lecture,
And go for Helen, Hecuba, and Hector.

For is not Tenedos in view, and does
  Not woody Ida in the distance lift
Her dim crest like a thunder-cloud, and flows
  Not lone Scamander where the sea-sands shift
And roars the surf, beyond whose surge the Greek
Moors, as ere *Ilium fuit*,[2] his caïque?

Would thou hadst ears, speech, intellect! As 'tis,
  I lock thee in my scrutoire, there to sleep
Till classed—a theme for erudite surmise
  And sage remark beyond the Western deep—
With skeletons of mammoths, mermaids, mummies,
Brickbats from Babylon, and other dummies.

---

[1] Called "The tomb of Ajax." In honor of him Alexander the Great is said to have run round it thrice naked, "which," says Lady Mary, in her "Oriental Letters," "was no doubt a great comfort to his ghost."

[2] Fuit Ilium.—*Virg.*

LAMENT OF THE EMIGRATING INDIAN.

HERE dwelt my tribe : these wooded hills,
　　These grassy plains were ours,
This forest with its lakes and streams,
Its game, its fruits, and flowers.
'Twill fall before the white man's stroke,
Like my own banished race,
Nor tree, nor stone, be left to mark
Our home, or burial-place.

The rifle of the settler, where
The red man roved, now rings :
Unheard his warwhoop, in his trail
The grass untrodden springs.
Beneath his hearth-stone breeds the snake,
The wild weeds o'er it wave ;
The bones are broken by the plough,
And driven from his grave.

Cold are our hearth-stones, desolate ;
Their smoke has passed away :

Moss-grown they moulder by the lake,
Where quenched their brands decay.
Then let us go! to wilds untamed
The wolf and panther flee :
The white man's home is for the slave,
The red man's for the free.

TO A FLOWER FROM THE ATHENIAN ACROPOLIS.

FRAIL, withered leaf! thy tints are shed,
    Thine odor scents a distant air;
No spirit here survives the dead,
    And seems to say, "The relic spare!"
Around me flowers in sunshine sleep,
    Whose dewy sweets arrest the bee,
Or blushing at my window peep,
    Yet do I turn from them to thee.

For thou wast cradled, nurtured, where
    The men, whose birth was Freedom's, rose;
There still survive their trophies, there
    The bones of heroes, gods,[1] repose;
Memorial of feelings high,
    As met the mount my awe-struck gaze,
Whose relics, though in dust they lie,
    Bespeak the pride of former days.

[1] Athenians deified, as Theseus and Erectheus.

Prized in remembrance of a spot
    Whose time-worn image haunts me still;
For who has marked, and e'er forgot
    The trophies of that glorious hill?
Still, though in shattered pride, elate,
    But soon to perish, like the flower
Sprung from the dust, that strews the seat,
    The monuments, of vanished power!

EVENING AT SEA.

THE stars, through falling dews that steep
    The shades of twilight, faintly shine,
And, though they weep not, seem to weep
    In silence o'er the day's decline;
O'er hours which vanish not, till they
    Promise more brightly to return;
But who for me, when gone for aye,
    Will mourn—nay, who will seem to mourn?

Perchance, upon a desert shore
    The sands shall heap my stoneless grave;
Perchance, above me heedless roar
    The thunder of the ocean-wave;
The wind, whose voice its breakers mock,
    Bear my last sigh unheard away;
The shadow of the mountain-rock,
    Forbid a flower to deck my clay.

And yet, so few my heart would own,
    Its memories prize, methinks that I,

Unheard, unwept, my dying moan
    Could calmly breathe to earth and sky.
My life is like yon orb, to rise
    Scarce dimly seen, lone, faint, and far;
And death to me may be as is
    The setting of that nameless star.

LOVE AND REASON.

SAID Venus, "Cupid! you're no more
   A child, to be with Hebe fooling;
Methinks you'd be, as well as she,
The better for a little schooling.
There's Ganymede, a boy no bigger
Than you are, beat him, if you can!
He sings and fiddles, rhymes and riddles,
In short, is quite the gentleman.

"I've had my day: Jove! how these fogs
And bleak winds of Olympus rack us!
Mars ogles less than he was wont,
And Vulcan[1] spends his nights with Bacchus:
To leave you helpless to your kin,
Or step-dame, should he wed, were cruel:
I'm posed to think how you'll contrive,
When I'm defunct, to earn your gruel.

"I'm told there dwells, somewhere about
Parnasse, a nymph, hight Reason, famed

[1] Her husband.

For brats like you, that better love
Their pastimes than their books reclaimed,
For fasting, single life, and vigils;
And, what will better serve, as *you* know,
To make you mind your Greek and morals,
She's uglier than that vixen Juno.

" We'll put you with her for a month—
A week for prose, and three for rhyme:
I learned to pen a billet-doux,
And thrum a lute, in half the time.
I'll straight dispatch my dove, to tell her
You'll make one of her bookish crew;
So take your wing, but leave your quiver,
The sight of it might fright the ' blue.' "

He went. The dame was busy with
Her wonted round of freakish fancies;
At length thought she, I'll go and see
How Cupid with the nymph advances.
The night was rough; said Venus, " Sure
They'll not be out, this stormy weather.
The door not fast? Within there, ho ! "—
Reason and Love had fled together.

The pupil now the teacher plays;
The nymph's Socratic nights are o'er;
Upon her centre-table lie
The tales of Ovid, songs of Moore.

No crabbed, ethic tome illumes
Her midnight lamp, but, supper done,
Love tunes her lute, and with her sings
From Sappho and Anacreon.

Comfits from either Ind her pantry,
Brooches and beads her cabinets fill:
"Surely," thinks Reason, "this is better
Than Plato, pulse, and dishabille."
She deems him, what he swears to be,
Her ever true and loving lord;
But soon the rogue is advertised
As having left her bed and board.

A bill is filed, and they are parted;
Neither to t'other much a debtor.
He to his champagne whistling goes,
She to her vigils and black-letter.
"Or young, or old," says Venus, "list!
Believe it! as if spoke by Jove,
Love ne'er was taught, or tamed by Reason,
And Reason never trust with Love!"

THE GLEN AND THE BURIAL.

A SCENE IN ANDRO, A GREEK ISLAND.

FROM morn our weary march had wound
  O'er heights by summer suns imbrowned;
At length at eventide, it fell
Into a wild, sequestered dell,
Where shrub and blossom seemed to dress
A hermitage for loneliness;
A dim retreat, where day the sprite
Had scarce disturbed, that walks at night;
As thither, since creation's birth,
Had come no living thing of earth,
But blossoms there, and trees, which shade—
  As watching o'er some hidden treasure—
Their shy, unscented sweets, had made
  A paradise for their own pleasure.
No sound was heard, save bleat of goat,
Or chime of convent-bell remote.

And rocks, no summer rills bedew,
  Like battlements in ruin proud,

Hung o'er it, with the fading hue,
   The stillness of an evening cloud:
A lone recess, where one, whose sigh
   Is but for peace and heaven, might come,
   Like a gray pilgrim to his home,
And feel 'twere happiness to die.[1]

Midway, along the steep, unworn
   By any track, a grassy plot
We found, by flock or scythe unshorn,
   And chose it for a burial spot.[2]
A stream—whose murmur, from the shade
Of wild vine-bower, or mossy grot,
The silence more impressive made—
Welled from a spring, so still and clear,
It seemed a nether hemisphere;
   A natural glass, wherein, I ween,
The nymph, if such there was, of tree,
   Or fountain-wave, might have been seen,
In ancient days and summer hours,
Knitting her tresses with the flowers,
A solitary tribe, we see
There woo the breeze and lure the bee,
Breathing, like nuns in silent prayer,
Their souls into the quiet air.

---

[1] The beauty of another valley, as seen by moonlight in this island, was such as to make the writer almost wish that he might never leave it.

[2] Of a marine officer, killed while we were crossing the island.

Few, but sincere, the rites we paid :
A stone, a wreath upon it laid
Of frail but fragrant flowerets, told
Where one, the battle-fire, though rolled
O'er many a broken rank, had spared,
Lay where no kindred sleeper shared
His low, lorn couch, unknown, forgot,
In a lone isle's most lonely spot.
And thrice the flashing volley woke
The echoes, thrice rang out their knell
Old wood and owlet-haunted rock—
A last and meet farewell!

TO YOUNG WOOD-ROSES.

FAIR flowers! your image, where the forest spring
    Sequestered sleeps, Narcissus-like that eye,
Well may the breeze, that fans with gentle wing
    Your odorous bloom, forsake it with a sigh!

Waving, as if to greet the early sun,
    Your tinctured kerchiefs, of his noontide ray
Beware! or, ere his evening race be run,
    You will have blown and withered in a day.

What mean your blushes, dewy tears, as now
    You lowly bend, with eyes half raised to heaven?
Baptized[1] we see you, but 'tis not, we know,
    Because, poor babes! you need to be forgiven.

You lowly bend, while we forget to kneel;
    Yet, ah! how many,[2] ere your sweets be blown,
May wish, too late, the shame you seem to feel,
    The tears you seem to shed, had been their own!

[1] Wet with dew.   [2] Of the dying.

SONNETS.

I.

MAY.

TO M———.

NOW heaven[1] seems one bright, rejoicing eye,
    And earth one flower. Blue violets recline
By bank or streamlet, imaging the sky,
    And the blown rose shames every cheek but thine;
The ground each moment, as some blossom springs,
    Or leaf unfolds, puts forth a lovelier dye,
Wooed by the bee, or west-wind's musky sigh,
And each new morning some new songster brings.
    And, hark! the brooks their rocky prisons break,
    And echo calls on echo to awake;
The air is rife with dewy sweets, and wings
    Rustling through wood, or dripping over lake.
Bird, bud, and leaf return, but not to me
With song or beauty, since they bring not thee.

[1] Though the lexicographers make this word a monosyllable, yet, as it cannot be pronounced but as a dissyllable, the writer, here and perhaps elsewhere, with a view to the measure, has ventured to regard it as such, as in one or more places does Tennyson at least, and also Spenser in the line—
"As the great eye of heaven shinèd bright."

II.

TO A YOUNG MOTHER.

WHAT things of thee may yield a semblance meet,
    And him, thy fairy portraiture? a flower
And bud, moon and attending star, a sweet
    Voice, and its sweeter echo. Time has small power
O'er features the mind moulds, and such, O shrine
Of truth and childlike gentleness! are thine,
    Imperishably lovely. Roses, where
They once have bloomed, a fragrance leave behind,
And harmony will linger on the wind,
    And suns continue to light up the air
When set, and garlands may the altar-stone,
    Though ruin claim the broken relic, twine;
Types of the beauty that, though youth be gone,
    Beams from the soul—nay, then may chiefly shine.

III.

TWILIGHT.—AT SEA, OFF DELOS.

SWEET is the hour to him that, on the sea,
    Far gleaming spies the solitary sail,
Or walks remote by woods, where folds the bee
    Her weary wing, and flowers the sweets exhale
    They hoard by day, and the lone night-bird's wail

Disturbs the echoes of the forest-wild;
   The hour, when winds are still, and stars are pale,
And earth and heaven seem once more reconciled.
   And, look! her blush steals on the dewy air,
Her silver girdle for the nightly chase
   As Dian belts, and, from her cloudy chair
O'er Cynthus,[1] smiles, with half-averted face,
   Her farewell to the sun. Long! ere the light
Of this calm eve shall set in memory's night.

IV.

CROSSING THE BEACH OF ABOUKIR BAY IN EGYPT.

THE moon is up, by light clouds swiftly past,
   Laden with tribute for the infant Nile;
Peeping, at times, from the ethereal waste,
   Some solitary star, with fitful smile,
   Trims her small lamp, whose beam may not beguile
The desert's loneliness; and on the shore,
   Aboukir's thundering surf untombs the pile—
The wave-worn relics it had earthed before.
Far other was the scene, the light, the roar,
   When, like a lurid meteor of the sky,

---

[1] This mountain, so called, remarkable as the reputed birthplace and hunting-ground of Apollo and Diana, we found to be a mere rocky hill of no very great elevation. They must have been satisfied with small game. The remains of the far-famed Delian temples the Greeks were converting into *lime!*

Nelson's red cross unfurled its death-sign o'er
   The astonished Gaul,[1] or he,[2] whose white plume high,
Still, like a standard, led the van of fight,
Headlong careering, smote the Ottomite.

V.

NAPOLEON.[3]

PAUSE! for a spirit still pervades the spot,
   A power by dull Oblivion's wand unlaid—
The memory of him, whose name to blot
   Time must despair, and whose imperial shade
Yet awes the world; his goal a lonely isle,[4]
   But course, the comet's, that, its meteor-car
Urging from some remote abyss, the while
It rushes onward, kindles from a star
Of twinkling lustre to a sunlike flame,
   And from its "hair shakes pestilence and war,"
Firing the firmament; to whom kings came
   And sued as bondmen, at whose feet were laid
   Nations in chains, whose eagles were displayed
Till earth became a camp, and right a name.

---

[1] The battle of the Nile was fought in this bay.

[2] Murat in the battle of Aboukir, who here made one of his most celebrated charges. Before it began, Bonaparte said to him, "This battle will decide the fate of the world." Murat replied, "Of the army at least." The Turks were defeated with a loss of twenty thousand men.

[3] Who here fought the battle of Aboukir.   [4] St. Helena.

VI.

RECOLLECTIONS OF GREECE.

'TWAS late my lot to tread those ancient shores,
    Where now the Spirit of old inspiration
Mourns by the fount whose Nymph no longer pours
    A hallowed stream; and of a mighty nation—
Stemming in story, as the eagle soars
    Against the wind, the ebbing stream of time—
To mark the mountain birthplace and the grave;
    The home of freedom trodden by the slave;
The ruinous dwelling of that soul sublime,
Whose voice is silent now, on shore and wave,
    As it had never sounded—a mute thunder!
    But not the less we pause, in silent wonder,
By tomb, or temple, or old stream, or dell,
Where poet mused, sage thought, or patriot fell.

VII.

ABSENCE.

I GATHERED many flowers of many tints—
    Roses that blush like innocence suspected
In maiden cheeks; the coinage Flora mints,
    Bright marigolds; narcissus-cups, reflected
By cold fount-wells; tulips, more gayly drest
    Than May-day queens; soft-eyed anemones;

And lilies whiter than e'er shamed the breast
  Of infant Dian, or the snow-flake. These
  Chose I, to please, if any thing might please,
As with thy portraiture, my loneliness;
  The fairest chose, as images of thee,
Nor vainly fair, had they been like thee less;
  But soon I found my sole relief must be,
Not emblems of thee, but forgetfulness.

VIII.

TO THE AUTHOR OF THE "LIFE OF ASHMUN."

THY task is o'er, a monument thou here
  Hast built, wherein the memory of him,
Whose tribute rightly were a nation's tear,
  Shall, like a star no earth-born vapors dim,
Survive, embalmed like relics in perfumes,
Or regal dust in Cyclopean tombs.
  I met thee in life's early day, and still
Have watched thy course—too long, through years gone by,
  Stealing unheard, yet, as the Alpine rill
Swells to the torrent, destined to a high
  And loud celebrity, the glorious crown
He wins, who strives truth, virtue, to promote;
  And long shall Afric in her heart enthrone
Thy worth, thy words long treasure in her thought.

IX.

TO THE PAINTER OF THE PANORAMA OF QUEBEC.[1]

PAINTERS we have, that, like the Florentine
   Or Flemish pencil, visions may have caught,
Of which the lifelike portraitures, once seen,
   Forever haunt us, seem with feeling fraught,
Nay, breath, nor picture only form, but thought :
Yet do we turn from them, and own the power
   Of Nature—clear, blue heaven, or grassy lap
Where sleeps the still lake in its forest-bower,
   Time-mantled peak, upon whose mossy cap
The snow, untouched by Summer, lies, whose breast
The gorgeous draperies Autumn weaves invest :
   But thou hast seized her pencil, and so true
Portrayed her, in her Northern colors drest,
   Sombre, or soft, that them in thine we view.

X.

SCIO.

PASS we the peak, by summer suns imbrowned ;
   The headland, imaged by the quiet deep
Dim, distant isles, like clouds reposing, bound ;
   The ruin, watch-tower, beetling o'er the steep ;

---

[1] The late distinguished landscape-painter, Richard R. Gibson, of Washington, D. C.

And lo ! a spot as of enchanted ground !
  O gracious God ! that we, as here, should see
Thy fairest works by human hand defaced ![1]
  Look on this Eden of the bird and bee !
Where Love, 'twould seem, his paradise had placed;
Yet here the Moslem, dull, as in a waste,
  Like tiger from the relics of his prey
Unroused, by no avenging weapon chased,
  Must make a solitude, where Nature, gay
With bird and blossom, makes a holiday.

XI.

LOVE OF SPIRITUAL BEAUTY.

RESTORE thy blush unto the summer rose,
  Thine eye, so softly shadowy, darkly bright,
Unto the twilight, hair unto the night,
Neck to the lily, forehead to the snows,

---

[1] This island, when visited by the writer, had but partially recovered from the devastation which accompanied the massacre at the commencement of the Greek Revolution. It was formerly called "The Paradise of the Islands," and appears to have been a favorite place of residence, even with some Europeans.

We visited the relic called "*The School of Homer*" (there being a tradition that he there taught poetry and music), but missed the statue mentioned in the subjoined notice of it by Chandler: "It appears to have been an open temple of Cybele, formed on the top of a rock. In the centre is the image of the goddess, the head and an arm wanting. She is represented as sitting. The chair has a lion carved on each side, and on the back."

Either in this island, or in the vicinity of Smyrna, Homer was probably born.

Hand—that no jewel but itself needs wear—
To Cupid's statue, for 'twill shame its white
And, like the stone's, is infantinely fair;
Thy breath to incense by the vernal air
Borne from some bower of Araby, thy lips
To half-blown pink-buds, sweets, of which the bee
Of those that scent the morning earliest sips.
All are but ornaments, not parts, of thee.
I woo not them, whate'er their loveliness:
I woo the soul, and they it do but dress.

XII.

THE GRAVE OF FITZ-GREENE HALLECK.[1]

Read at the dedication of his monument in Guilford, Connecticut, 8th July, 1869.

IN thee no gorgeous capital, no mart,
Known wheresoe'er a wave rolls, though we see,
Yet, Guilford, even thine no humble part
In memory's pageant henceforth e'er shall be.
The earth that heaps thy relics, Halleck, where
No name more famed sepulchral shaft shall bear,
Full many a pilgrim-bard from many a shore
Shall wend to greet, till time shall be no more;
The spot, henceforth to genius ever dear,
Shall gladly hail nor quit without a tear;

[1] See the first note to the piece entitled "Idlings with Nature."

Some strain of thy imperishable lyre
Recall, and, ere reluctant he retire,
Exclaim, "In thee, O Fame's lamented son!
A thousand poets we have lost in one."

XIII.

SCENE REVISITED AFTER THE DEATH OF A FRIEND.

A SNOW-WHITE beach, a narrow path, that winds,
   Like a foam-ripple, by the river-wave,
O'erhung with cedars and cone-dropping pines:
   And, see! the stream lies couched, as in a cave,
In this lone nook, and wears his lily-crown,[1]
Disturbed but by the water-king,[2] that down
   Darts, as if bent to battle with his peer,
The shape, with sword-like beak and bristling crest,
   That ever mocks him, imaged in the clear
Still flood, the semblance of a sky at rest.
   But where is she, whose gentle footsteps seem
Yet uneffaced, since, arm in arm, we went
   By this calm water? vanished! as a dream,
A star that melts into the firmament.

[1] The water-lily.   [2] The kingfisher bird.

EARLY SPRING.

A S yet, no blossoms by the rill
   And sheltering hill-side, peep :
Herbage and earlier wood-flower, till
   The bluebird wakes them, sleep.
He comes! the messenger of Spring,
   With his glad minstrelsy,
And bearing in his herald wing
   The tincture of her sky.

Soon, as before fresh dews and flowers
   Shall strew the lap of May;
How unlike gone and happier hours
   That bid farewell for aye !
Sweet minstrel! doubly sweet, might I,
   Like thee, those hours forget;
As 'tis, I listen with a sigh,
   A feeling of regret.

THE MARINER'S FAREWELL.

THE cape is cleared, before us lies
   Our path, the bright blue main;
The land fades far,
   And cord and spar
The swelling topsails strain;
Our good ship bounds before the breeze,
That freshens fast and fair,
   And skims the sea
   As light and free,
As if she moved in air.

One mute farewell, one look, as, where
The blue sky meets the foam,
   Headland and isle
   Fast fade the while,
Then proudly greet our home!
   No care have we,
   So winds blow free
And fair, my merry crew!
And, hark! the sea-bird bids good-night—
   Our native land, adieu!

AUTUMN IN GREECE.

AROUND me are the relics sad
   Of Hellas in her palmy hour;
O'er which the weeds, that sighing fade
   Or silent droop, their dead leaves shower.
I look forth upon shore and sea,
   Dim, distant isles, and cloudless skies,
And all is lone, as it should be,
   Where Ruin dwells, and Nature dies.

I see with fainter colors glow
   Hills, late by vernal blossoms crowned;
I hear the wind, with whisper low,
   Its farewell fragrance breathe around;
The lizard, through the long, dry fern,
   Darts rustling, and her dewy pall
The spider spreads o'er rifled urn,
   O'er leafless brake, and prostrate wall.

I note the few, pale, drooping flowers,
   That loiter by the green hill-side:

Unprized their sweets, the bee to bowers
    And fields of richer bloom has hied;
I see their cups with cold dews wet,
    And feel the fading wreath, they twine
For Autumn's brow, so few, as yet,
    My joyous hours, were meet for mine.

By bank and brake the bird flits lone,
    With fitful note, no longer glad;
Like his, my early mates are gone,
    Like his, my song is low and sad;
Too deeply sad, where Empire's grave
    And Nature's but of ruin tell;
Where summer flowers no longer wave,
    And autumn's seem to sigh farewell.

SONG OF THE GRECIAN YOUTH.

Illustrating a representation of a maiden, presenting a goblet and garland to a Grecian youth.

FILL not for me the cup with wine!
It sparkles like thine eye;
For me no wreath of roses twine!
They breathe but of thy sigh.
But pledge me in oblivion's wave,
And I will drink to thee;
And of a sleepy fragrance let
The wreath, you weave me, be.

Of night-blown poppies weave the wreath,
With dews of Lethe wet!
For though 'tis sweet to think of thee,
'Twere sweeter to forget.
It is not wine that can efface
Thy image from my brain;
But pledge me in oblivion's wave,
And I the cup will drain.

CAPE COLONNA, IN GREECE.

"Save where Tritonia's airy shrine adorns
Colonna's cliff, and gleams along the wave."
Byron.

'TIS summer's eve. The winds are still,
So calmly hushed the waters lie,
So softly bright, they seem to blend
In airy distance with the sky.
What gorgeous hues of beauty, o'er
Laconia's hills and mountains rolled,
Their summits veil! where sinks the sun,
A monarch to his couch of gold.
From them I turn, from isles, along
Whose wild and dusky outlines driven,
The rosy twilight fades, till light
Their starry fires the watch of heaven;
Turn to the ruin,[1] lone and dim,
That bears the name, and should have crowned,
By sea-dews wept, the dust of him [2]

[1] Remains of the temple of Minerva Sunias.
[2] Byron, whose name we found there inscribed. This cape was the scene of Falconer's poem, "The Shipwreck." The beauty of the view from it, on a calm summer evening, like that on which we visited it, has perhaps hardly a parallel. We subsequently met with an Albanian, who said he had

Whose song, though mute, seems breathed around.
Chieftain ! whose call, by sea and shore,
The men of Greece in arms obeyed;
Soldier ! whose charge had led them where
Shall foremost wave her battle-blade,
Here should thy relics rest, beside
This time-worn ruin, gray and rent,
Thy name thy epitaph, the stone,
That name inscribes, thy monument.

been one of Byron's soldiers, and spoke of him with much enthusiasm, slapping his breast, looking heavenward, and exclaiming, "*Beerom! Beerom!*" as he called him. At another time, having landed at a lonely place below Smyrna, we were accosted by a poor fellow who, in broken English, said that he had been a servant of Byron, and was with him when he died. He described his person correctly, and spoke of him with tears. He was a deserter from an Austrian man-of-war, and begged to be taken to our ship, a favor that, because he was such, was unfortunately quite inadmissible. The thought subsequently occurred that possibly he was the "*Tite,*" a foreign servant, who is mentioned as having been with the poet in Greece.

TO A WITHERED ROSE FROM THE BANKS OF THE MELES.[1]

THOU mind'st me when by banks we strayed,
    The oleander made one flower,
And spied thee, dripping in their shade,
    A Naiad in her bower;

With dewy, downcast eye, and cheek,
    That half a blush disclosed—a thing
Betwixt a bud and blossom, meek,
    Young daughter of the Spring;

With breath, that had betrayed, unspied,
    Thy lurking-place, tempting the bee,
In search of other sweets, aside
    To steal a kiss from thee,

And me, as, shrinking at my feet,
    Thy dewy eye looked up to mine,

[1] On the banks of this small but beautiful river, and in the vicinity of Smyrna, Homer is said to have been born, while his mother was present at some rural festival. Hence he was called *Melesigenes*. See a translation prefixed to Buckley's "Odyssey," of a very curious and, if authentic, interesting notice of him, ascribed to Herodotus.

To leave thee to thy mossy seat,
   And canopy of vine.

Go! relic of a faded wreath,
   Bid her, to whom I send thee, o'er
Thy dead leaf sigh! and it will breathe
   More sweetly than before.

THE SELF-EXILED'S FAREWELL.

In this and the next piece, the author is supposed to personate, not himself, but an unfortunate friend, on his leaving the country, and returning to it after an absence of some years.

BRIGHT are your skies, no lovelier bend
   O'er the blossoms and fruits of the year;
And if Liberty e'er found a home, or a friend,
   But where man is a stranger, 'tis here.
But the spirit from tyrants has little to fear,
   In the pride of her apathy free;
And with few years before me, to sadden or cheer,
   My lone path I trace o'er the sea.

To the land of the olive, the orange, and vine,
   Of the rose, and the nightingale's song,
Scenes seeming of Eden—they soothe not a mind
   That but broods over sorrow and wrong.
'Tis the land whose gone glories in memory live
   Like the twilight her summer eves cast,
And where he, whom the present has little to give,
   Communion may hold with the past:

May pause and may ponder by ruins, that moan
  To the wind, as complaining of Time,
Or, if mute, like the spirit that, stern and alone,
  Stands hushed in her grief and sublime.
They hear not, they speak not, and yet, in their face
  And their echoes, a look and a tone
The forsaken, the friendless, may fancy they trace—
  A feeling, a fate, like their own.

But the white sail is set, and our ship flings the foam,
  Like a courser that chafes to be free :
Farewell bids the sea-bird; e'en she has a home,
  But, my spirit! where smiles it for thee?
Shall I go to the spot where my forefathers sleep,
  Halls but to the stranger now known?
No eye there is left me to smile, or to weep;
  Let the wind, let the wave, waft me on !

THE SELF-EXILED'S RETURN.[1]

THE land is made, the port is nigh,
   But dark and chill the wintry sky,
Not the deep blue, the golden hue,
   Of climes late left, where summer hours
Returning suns so soon renew,
   We hardly miss their vanished flowers.
And, though old rock, and woodland cape,
And beacon-tower, with airy shape,
Seem, coming swiftly up from ocean,
To greet us with a joyous motion,
And the wild scream of the sea-mew
Be like a welcome rude, but true—
I heed them not; unfelt they come
To him, for whom there waits no home,
No tear, no smile, whose sympathy
He haply feels, or cares should be;
No hand, perchance, whose greetings tell
The lips were true that sighed farewell.
For I am as the drift I see

---

[1] See note prefixed to the piece next preceding this.

The surge, to where it grew, return,
And earth alike and ocean spurn.
My childhood hearth is desolate,
   Or trod alone by stranger feet;
Nor sister more, nor early mate,
   My coming there with smiles shall greet.
Unprized, perhaps, or gone are all
   Mine eye there met, my heart held dear.
The feelings I may not recall
   Of hours remembered with a tear.
   If thither led, 'twill be to hear
No kindred voices, to behold
No features but the changed or cold.

IDLINGS WITH NATURE.[1]

CRADLED among the wild sequestered hills,
A stream of such small note as haply wins
Some village beauty in her rural home,
With quiet wave meanders to the sea.
From mere, reflected by whose willowy pool
The heron meditates, it issuing winds
By grassy slope and woodland shade obscure,
Where, neophyte in Greek, but deeply versed
In tongues wherewith the pupils Nature schools—
Winds, waters, and the wingèd choirs—commune,
I spent my happier, and, if truant oft
To lettered for her pictured volume, yet

[1] Entitled, in a former edition, "Rambles in Autumn." The descriptive parts of this piece relate chiefly to a beautiful valley and its environs—at least as they were in the author's early days—in the township of Guilford, Connecticut. A portion of the woods belonged to the mother of Halleck, the poet, and therefore was doubtless familiar to him in his boyhood. In a cemetery, at the head of this valley, stands his monument (dedicated on the 8th of July, 1869), a costly and beautiful structure, for which the township is indebted chiefly to the exertions of his friend and biographer, General James Grant Wilson, of the city of New York.

Perchance my not least profitable hours;—
Recumbent, through the long, lone summer-day,
With other vagrant elf, in green-wood shade,
Or—if at times roused to more active sport—
Like the great children of the busy world,
Pursuing what we either saw elude
Our grasp, or, haply, disappoint if won—
Now the gay butterfly, now glancing where
Her wing out-hummed the bee, the bird[1] whose plumes
Seem borrowed of the rainbow, or the tints
Of every flower that hives for her its sweets.

Into the meadows from the woodland hills
At intervals projecting may be seen
A long, low cape of verdant upland, crowned
At its extremity with beech and oak,
As 'twere a veteran outpost, planted there
To watch and check incursions of the stream;
Who, swollen at certain changes of the moon,
Like lunatic that deems himself a king,
Quits his scant channel, as he did disdain
The crown of tributary sedge he strews,
Flooding his banks. And, looking oceanward,
A ledge, at times, of old fantastic rock
Lifts its huge form, with trees of knotty growth
Shot slanting from its briery clefts, profuse
Of unpruned shrub, of vine and flower, that shun

[1] Humming-bird.

The cultured walk, and, nun-like, seem to trim
Their lone retreat for no eye but their own—
The bramble, that the purple berry, like
A ruby in a wood-nymph's chaplet, wears;
Sumachs, whose scarlet shames the conchs of Tyre;
Deep-dyed lobelia,[1] gorgeous as a bride
Of Ind, and firing with her torch the gloom
Alder or other growth of dark, dull leaf,
As envious of her queenlike beauty, sheds;
Bright constellations of red columbines,
Like ear-drops pendent from the fern-fringed edge
Of rock, in whose dun shade, as fearful lest
Some eye should note her sweets, the violet lurks;
The golden lily with her speckled cup;
The meadow-pink, waving her crimson cap;
Frail wind-flowers, that their snowy kerchiefs spread
To shield their beauty from the April air;
The flaunting ivy,[2] thrusting forth her bloom,
Like village maid vain of her charms; the brier,[3]
Whose rose out-scents the Arabian spring; and, rare,
Some shy, cold blossom, Flora's nun, that loves
To hide her blushing beauty from the world,
And die unseen—lone dwellers of the rough
And tangled ways, with which we sympathize,
As things, though beautiful and not without
A seeming sense of their own loveliness,

---

[1] The cardinal-flower.
[2] The common misnomer, as also is "laurel," of a species of *Kalmia*.
[3] Sweetbrier.

That spring, and bloom, and to their graves go down,
Like humble worth, unnoticed and unwept.

And far beyond and at the valley's head,
Frowns o'er the scene a forest of old trees,
Dusky, and printing on the northern sky
His shaggy outline, nor less crowns the hills,
On this side, rocky, high, and rudely piled,
On that, with lazy slope, grassy and green;
Both stretching towards the ocean, till they end,
Like headlands, in the sea-like meadow flats.

It is a spot where I have spent the hours
We feel the least reluctance to recall.
There did my boyhood sport, or idly gaze
Upon the still and gorgeous scenery
Of wood, and sky, and clouds in whose bright shapes
It feigned a world of airy images,
Gay shapes of living things, castles and spires,
Turrets and battlements, and gilded roofs—
All I had pictured of old fairy-land—
And sighed (if boy may sigh) to see them fade,
And think they were too beautiful to last.
There did I lie, seeking the thickest shade
By wild vine thrown, and let the noontide scene
Impress me, passive as the stream whose face
I saw its dream-like imagery reflect;
Or haply watched the eagle—with my hand

Shading my eye, as, wheeling slow, he soared
Till dwindled to a speck or turned to air—
And longed to have his wing, wherewith, at will,
To roam those wondrous regions, and to visit
Far distant lands, whereof I heard strange tales,
And some, I live to find, more strange than true.

It was among my earliest haunts and last,
That solitary vale, and, ere I bade
What seemed must be a long farewell to home,
I spent a day of rambling there, to dwell
Once more upon its features, as I would
Upon a friend's, so long known and so loved
He wellnigh seems a portion of myself.

It was a morn in autumn, such as, ere
The first snow falls, like a pleased guest returns,
Once more to smile a bright, but brief farewell.
The web hung without motion from the tree;
The down, that, shaken from the thistle-top,
Stood tiptoe, rose not into the still air;
And, freighted with the caterpillar, rolled
In her silk shroud, the willow leaf had dropped,
And lay at anchor on the pool, which seemed
The thing it imaged—an inverted heaven.
The fox had to his covert slunk, and left
The cock to strut amid his dames secure,
Though the dew told where late his foot had been,

And a low baying, where the far-off hills
Rose wooded, that the hound was on his track.
The eagle shook the hoar-frost from his wing,
And, soaring, faced a sun without a cloud;
And a faint haziness, as it had been
A white transparent veil, flung o'er a nun
Bending in worship at the altar, lent
A deeper softness and solemnity
To scenes, though gorgeous as the trains the East
Sees sweep the bannered aisles that urn her kings,
Yet sad as they; woods, in whose fading pomp,
Though summer cheered them with a lingering smile
And hung upon their sheltered skirts, was read
To her gay pensioners a sad farewell.
A brook-side loiterer, the wood-rose, had
Tendered her sweets, and, with a blush, retired;
Her sapphire crown the gentian wore, but stood
Hourly prepared to cast her robe and die;
The butterfly her wing, bedropped with gold,
Had folded till some kindlier sun's return;
The breeze, that haunts the river-marge and chants
A drowsy song among the reeds, lay hushed;
The woodland thrush his pipe of many stops—
No longer at Aurora's window heard
Long ere she left her bed—had closed, or made
No more nor better music than the crow,
The sentinel that, from the topmost bough
Of an old oak, whose frown imbrowned the dell,
With cry discordant challenged my approach.

So, in the bright, warm sunshine venturing forth,
With no companion but a friend, my dog,
I took a skiff, and let the quiet flood
Of that lone stream drift me along, at times
Dipping my oar, thereby to shun some cape
Or reef of sand, or headland of shell-bank.
Now from some log, on which he basked, or shelf,
A tortoise dropped, or prowling muskrat dived,
Whisking, as if with mischievous intent,
The blinding spray-drops, from his whip-like tail,
Into my eyes; or, from the reeds would spring,
Whirring, the meadow-wren, or, lighting, start
And stare and sputter from their bending tops,
As if indignant and no less amazed
That I, with causeless and ill-timed approach,
Should thus upon the privacy intrude
And urgent duties of her precious life;
Or meditative heron, perched, where lay
The mouldering wreck of some old hulk, half sunk
And strewn with barnacles, would slowly thrust
Above the sedge, his long, lank neck, then crouch,
Till, floundering upward with an awkward flap
Of his dank wing, and knot of sea-grass seen
Dangling from his long legs, he slowly urged
His flight to stream or shallow, more remote:
Or crow, caught sleeping at his morning watch,
Bestirred himself and called, ere well awake,
Unto his fellows, that, with clamorous cry,
Rose, and their train winged lengthening to the wood.

Thus sped my voyage of small adventure, till,
Borne quietly along, far up the stream,
I cast a few links of a rusty chain
Over my paddle, thrust into the bank,
And upward strolled to where dismantled stood
An ancient domicile, beneath the frown
Of a tall wood of aged walnut-trees :
As if some ghost, that haunted their dim shade,
Had ventured forth, to breathe the purer air
And feel the blessèd sun. A relic lorn
Of simpler, if not better, days it seemed,
Not unfrequented by its ancient guest,
The swallow, but forsaken by the rat,
Like a poor client by his counsellor,
And wearing, in its riven front, the marks
Of other thievish hand than that of time.
Strange faces, if old legends rightly tell,
Stared at the paneless windows, voices strange,
At twilight, by the forester, as lone
He homeward hied, were heard, till all aghast
He stood the wondering family before,
Speechless and telling, in his looks, his tale.
Like other infidels, we laughed and still
Believed, and gathered in an idle group
Of vagrant urchins, where the bough of yon
Old oak the summer fount-well shaded, listened
To one, more grave and knowing than the rest,
Who, heard with gaping wonder, much discoursed
Of things of high inquiry in old days,

Witches, and ghosts, and armies in the sky,
And pots of buried gold that sank when struck,
Watched by the grisly phantom of old Kidd,[1]
With rusty pistol stuck beneath his belt,
And blood-stained hanger, through which, as it waved,
Glimmered the moon, as it had been of air!
The tree remains: that philosophic lout
And his co-truant sect, Peripatetics
Of Nature's good old school, the fields and woods,
Shy of her teachings if set forth in Greek,
But deeply versed in her unlettered lore,
In tongues of insects, rivulets and birds,—
Where are they now? The flowers of other lands,
Unconscious mourners, dew the graves of some,
And some, perchance the happier few, have found
A simple, but not nameless, stone, beside
The turf that heaves o'er their ancestral dust:
Others, like me, still wander on, to find
Not vainly did the ancients picture Hope
With hand that held a half-blown flower, with wing
Lifted, as she would ever fly, and foot
But touching earth, as it were not her home.
Among them there was one, beside the door
Of the old mansion of whose boyhood grew
Two willows, in whose still shade he was wont

---

[1] Within a few miles of the scene of this poem, is a beautiful group of islets called "The Thimbles," which this reputed outlaw is said to have frequented, and where formerly it was customary to dig for his supposed buried, treasures, amid, report says, showers of stones from the witches who guarded them. They are a fit domain for Oberon and his Queen.

Outstretched to lie, through the long summer days,
And dream of much 'twas then and since has been
His aim, but not his lot, to realize.
Years came, at length, of less impassioned hope,
And he had wandered long, and Nature wooed
In all, but, chiefly, her sequestered haunts
With an unweanèd fondness; shunned his kind,
And, smitten with her unveiled loveliness,
Sought her by stream, in wood, by ocean-wave,
Where'er he traced few steps of man, but she
In God's undesecrated presence dwelt,
And of his wisdom, power, and goodness spake.
He had stored his mind, too, with ideal shapes—
The grand and beautiful, the dark and bright
Of Fancy's realm. The ruins of old days—
The skeletons of empire's sepulchre—
Had glared upon him, with their thunder-scarred
And spectral aspects, fittest to inspire
Thoughts deep and unforgotten. And yet ne'er
Saw he, in all his wanderings, or felt
Aught to forbid sad longings for the hours
He spent, a boy, recumbent in the shade
Of those two willows; sad he sees them still,
Imaged as tangible, to his mind's eye,
As when, in spring, they put forth their green leaves,
Scenting, at morn, the dewy air with balm,
Or echoing to the hum of noontide bee.

IDLINGS WITH NATURE.

Reaching the skirts of the old wood, I paused,
Suffering the quiet beauty of the hour,
With all its soft, but bright serenity,
The place, with all its gorgeous scenery
Of fading forest hues—rich light and shade,
To fit me, passive, for that idle mood
Of dreaming wakefulness, in which I've spent
Much of what haply the great world might call,
And perchance rightly, a most worthless life.

All was so still that I could almost count
The tinklings of the falling leaves, the low,
Faint sounds, that knell them, by their fellow-dead
Of last year's growth borne, dew-wept, to their graves.
At times, indeed, detached by its own weight,
A nut would drop, and then, as if it had
His grasp eluded as he struck the meat,
Was heard a squirrel's short and fretful bark.
Anon, a troop of noisy, roving jays,
Whisking their gaudy topknots, would surprise
And seize, with sudden swoop, on some tall tree,
Shrieking, as if on purpose to enjoy
The consternation of the lone, still noon.
Roused by the din, with solemn hoot, the owl,
Like some grave justice bent to keep the peace,
Indignant stared, much wondering what it meant.
And on a stone there, near me, basked a fly
In the warm sunshine, vain of his green coat
Of variable velvet, laced with gold,

That, ever and anon, would whisk about,
Vexing the stillness with his buzzing din,
As human fopling will do with his talk;
And o'er the mossy post of an old fence,
Lured from its crannies by the warmth, was spied
A swarm of gay motes, waltzing to a tune
Of their own humming; or some cricket, which
The last night's frost had spared, crept feebly forth,
And, sadly merry, piped one carol more.

Round the old tenement, toward which I drew
With a strange thrill, that made me gladly feel
And closely strain the oakling in my grasp,
And swing it with an air of courage, all
At noonday, as at midnight, lone, was still;
Save that, at intervals, a door, which seemed
By hand invisible disturbed, would creak,
Or window-frame, mysteriously jar.
A toad sat musing on the mouldering sill,
And, planted on a post, was seen to bleach
What seemed the skull of some departed steed;
A withered weed, to me of name unknown,
Shot from each eyeless socket, and, where once
Had been an ear, her web the spider spun.

A few old, straggling posts, half sunk in earth,
And alleys, edged with stinted boxwood, told
Where once had been a garden. The rank sward,
Brambles and weeds, the savage hordes that press

Defenceless culture from her flowery walks,
Had o'errun bed and bower, trampling each plant
Of delicate and artificial growth,
Save where, perchance, with look half wild, half tame,
Some fruit-tree sapling battled for the soil
Of his more civilized progenitors;
Or straggling honeysuckle, or rose-bush—
The fragrance of whose sere leaf, like a sigh,
Stole on the sense and else unscented air—
Seemed gently to implore the passer-by
And crave a rescue from intruding thorns:—
All but the sunflower; she, in gorgeous trim,
With queen-like air, rose stately and apart,
And proudly wore her diadem of gold,
And bent not but in worship to her love.

In front, an agèd oak his knotted, gnarled
And mossy branches threw forth with an air
Of battle and defiance to the winds,
That, for a century, had swept his leaves,
But not his strength, to oblivion and decay:—
A type of Virtue warring against Fortune,
Shorn of the honors that the world confers,
Thence unimpaired, and bending to the stroke
Alone of Heaven. Like a sepulchral shaft,
With names misspelt, or indecipherable,
(Emblem of much ambition leaves to time,)
His trunk was scored, and, midway planted, wore

A rusty horseshoe, antidote, whilom,
To stroke of star malign and wizard spell.

Without, at either end, a chimney heaved
Its shapeless stack of no less shapeless stones,
Rent as by lightning, with dry knots of grass
And sticks of wrens' nests thrust in every chink.
Long! since the chattering tenant of the eaves
Had, at the lattice, as the day-star bade
His dewy farewell to the morning, peeped,
To greet the simple inmates; long! since curled
The quiet smoke from the old chimney-top,
Fragments of which lay mouldering on the roof,
With fern, or plant of like dull leaf, o'ergrown,
And moss, spungy and green, and, here and there,
A weed or toadstool sprouting from its tufts.

Nor had the nibbling, cankering tooth of time
Less busy been within. A door aslant,
Held by a single rusty hinge, revealed
A passage, trailing at whose entrance waved
A cobweb, hung with carcasses of flies.
The scantlings of the floor were loose and warped,
And, here and there, a head of rusty nail
Had started from them. Wasp-combs on the wall
Warned the bee [1] elsewhere, if she would her sweets
See safely stored, to excavate her cell;

[1] The boring humblebee.

And, in a corner, was a squirrel's hole,
Through which long nettles shot toward the light,
And, peeping forth, the husk of an old ear
Of corn betrayed the pilferer, and shells
Of mouldy nuts were strewn about its edge;
And, on the sunken hearth-stone, beneath whose
Gray slab he burrowed, lay a half-burnt brand,
And fragments of a chimney-swallow's nest.

   The field-mouse, from his summer home dislodged,
With wary forecast had been busy where
Dank, mouldering masses of coarse meadow-grass
Stood, smoking in the sun; at one of which
A half-grown, unshorn outlaw of a steer
Was planted, goring, with his short, sharp horns,
The mouldy fodder, which he tossed and snuffed
Indignant, heedless that his wrath unhoused
A luckless weasel and her helpless brood.
At sight of me he paused, and, pricking forth
His shaggy ears, advanced with look, as 'twere,
Of battle and defiance, but, in sooth,
Of perturbation and mute wonder. Man
To him seemed doubtless but a creature strange,
In whom he traced small semblance to his kind,
Nor aught to make him wish the distance less
That intervened betwixt him and my staff.
So there he stood, as spectre-stricken, till
My dog came loitering up from some dull scent
Of game he haply sought not, and, anon,

Dismissed him headlong to where wondering gazed
His fellow outlaws from the forest-shade.

    The lonely hours thus idly busy flew,
In that half-listless, half-observant mood,
When thoughts of serious or of sportive aim
Alike impress us, till the gorgeous west
Sunset lit up, with all the drapery
Wherewith she loves to deck her couch of clouds,
The last I've seen, and, haply, e'er shall see,
Sink o'er those hills and linger o'er those woods.

BATTLE OF SAN JACINTO IN TEXAS.

'TIS done, the sword is once more sheathed,
   So nobly drawn in valor's cause,
And Texas sees her soil bequeathed
   To freeborn men and equal laws;
Bequeathed by those who, whether they
   As victors or as vanquished fell,
Have left a deathless memory,
   A spirit that no might may quell.

The monuments of Freedom are
   The names of such; the scroll decays,
Nor less will time the marble spare
   Where Fame records their deeds and praise;
The names of those, whose swords have won,
   Redeemed the green sod where they lie,
Transmitted still from sire to son,
   From heart to heart, can never die.

And by their graves, in years to come,
    Where firm they stood, or rushed to greet
With shouts the foeman's trump and drum,
    He never more shall wind or beat,
Shall dwell a race, untaught to bow
    To tyrant power—a race, whose hands
Shall bear the flag—whose free folds now
    In triumph float—to other lands.

And there the sire, as the plough turns
    Some warlike relic from the sod,
Whose mould the battle-ranks inurns
    That few, but fearless, "blood-shod strode,"
Shall from it shake the dust, and turn
    And to the stripling proudly say,
Here firm we stood, there fell the foe
    On Texas' independence-day.

POETRY OF THE WOODS.

THE face of Nature, where it once has been
    Deeply impressed, remains indelible,
As does a mother's in the memory
Of an affectionate though weanèd child;
Earth, sea, and sky, have each their votaries,
Their worshipped forms, but ever forest depths
That house the eagle, and their giant trunks
See, unmolested by the woodman's stroke,
Ascend, or perish but by that of time.
And surely he—that, with rude foot, disturbs
The echoes, couched, like Dryads, in their shade,
And hears the wind prolong, through the deep gloom
Of their o'er-arching and wide-spreading boughs,
Its solemn music, and the low, strange sounds,
Uttered, as 'twere, from an unearthly shrine,
By powers invisible, and does not feel
The thrill of an imaginative awe,
A visionary consciousness of more
Than meets the sense—may well conclude, whate'er

The star that blessed his birth, 'twas none whose power
The Muse e'er felt or blessed. " Forbear!" had said
The nymphs, whose whispers heard the Delphic shades,
" Nor dare profane the Genius of the spot!"

THE FALL OF THE OAK—AN AUTUMN SCENE.

A GLORIOUS tree is the oak!
   He has stood for a thousand years,
  Has stood and frowned
  On the woods around,
Like a king among his peers.
As around their king they stand, so now,
   As the flowers their pale leaves fold,
The tall trees around him stand, arrayed
   In their robes of purple and gold.

The autumn sun looks kindly down;
  But the frost is on the lea,
   And sprinkles the horn
   Of the owl, at morn,
As she hies to the old oak-tree.
   Not a leaf is stirred,
   Not a sound is heard,

Save the thump of the thresher's flail,
    The low wind's sigh,
    Or the distant cry
Of the hound on the fox's trail.

By wild thorn-brake, and brook-marge green,
Winding his way, the woodman's seen,
    Till lost in the dewy gloom
      That shrouds the hill,
      Where, few and chill,
    The sunbeams struggling come;
Where the last flower scents the frosty air;
    And, hark! o'er height and hollow,
As the partridge whirs from her leafy lair,
    His strokes the echoes follow.

    Like a ship at sea,
    Rocks the old oak-tree;
Through the folds of his gorgeous vest,
    You may see him shake,
    And the night-owl break,
With a hoot, from his golden crest.
She will come but to find him gone from where
    He stood at the glimpse of day;
Like a cloud that peals, as it melts in air,
    He has passed, with a crash, away.

Though the spring in green, and the frost in gold,
  No more his limbs attire,
    The wild sea-wave
    He shall mount, and brave
  The blast and the battle-fire;
Shall spread his white wings to the wind,
    And thunder on the deep,
      As he thundered, ere
      His bough was bare,
    On the high and stormy steep.

RUINS OF THE TEMPLE OF JUPITER PANHELLENIUS,[1]

IN THE ISLAND OF ÆGINA.

LONE, from the summit of a lofty isle,
   The columns of a ruined temple lift
Their shattered fronts, each with its diadem
Of crumbling architrave and withered weeds.
A gray fraternity! rough with the dints
That speak of battle with the elements—
So old, indeed, and weather-stained, they seem
More ancient than the pinnacle they crown.

A proud and lofty structure in its day!
Peopled, perchance, with shapes of breathing stone,
And rich in sculpture of historic feats;
But, now, consisting of a few gray shafts,
That, by the winds, as sea-rocks by the waves,
Wasted, do yet, in their old aspects, wear
A look of majesty and stern command:

[1] "Of all the Greeks."

As if some Titan, battling with the gods,
Had perished, blasted in the very act
To dare their thunder, and there left his bones,
Upright, and bleaching in the mountain air.

Silent we stood in their lone noontide shade,
And only heard the bee's low hum, or chirp
Of the small martlet, that delights to build
And sport, as 'twere in mockery of man,
Where desolation has usurped his seat.

But in these old and time-worn relics, whose
Majestic columns—now the broken chords
Whose minstrel is the element—erewhile
Responded, with a loud, a lofty voice,
To festive or heroic argument,
And, hung with garlands, like a vernal grove,
Inhaled the incense, heard the vows, and were
The council-hall of universal Greece,
There dwells the spirit of a mightier spell,
Whose ministers are proud remembrances,
Linked by indissoluble sympathy
To human hearts—phantoms of haughty sway,
Warlike achievement, hazardous emprise,
Indomitable freedom, and the mind,
Whose light, though set, forever past, has left
A vivifying and creative power,
Felt and confessed throughout the universe.

LIFE.

A Parody on the "Battle of Hohenlinden."

WHEN life's young blood is felt to glow,
Bounding from finger-tip to toe,
As it were Bourbon or Bourdeaux,
    E'en but to *be* is jollity.

In our hope's sky then ever gay
Kaleidoscopic phantoms play;
Life is to be one summer day,
    The world, the land hight "Faèry."

But manhood comes, a stern, staid sprite;
O then to bright boy-dream good-night!
When things begin to black from white
    To change their May-morn livery.

If bachelors, we're lass-lorn, lone,
If husbands, bantlings, one by one,
With bakers, butchers, bills up-run,
    And wives with shops for finery.

Tax-gatherers, duns, a houndlike pack,
Law, quacks, our pockets, peace, still rack.
Each thinks himself, at last, a jack,[1]
    And with much reason generally.

Our better angel cries, "Repent!"
Our evil, "No!" till, earthward bent,
Haply misused each talent lent,
    We close life's tragi-comedy.

[1] An ass.

PIECES OF A RELIGIOUS CHARACTER.

I.

THE TWO WORLDS.

WHEN from the flower of life has fled
    The sweetness of its early bloom,
And, o'er its fading tints, are shed
    The dark, cold shadows of the tomb,
Oh! then for hopes we cease to care,
    That light us not to worlds on high,
But forms of seeming brightness wear,
    And, as we think to grasp them, fly.

When Pleasure o'er the cheerless cup,
    Whose dregs are tears, repentant sighs,
Its garlands dead, its wine drank up,
    And Love puts out his torch and dies,

Friendless and lone, by sorrow tried,
    Oh! then we turn, from earthly bliss,
To worlds where purer spirits bide,
    Beyond the false, cold smiles of this.

II.

THE PAST AND THE PRESENT.

TO C———.

WE met in other, brighter hours,
    When life seemed like the fabled isle,[1]
Whose spring ne'er cast her wreath of flowers,
    And sky was one, unclouded smile:
And we have found it like the strand,[2]
    Whose fruits are seen to tempt the eye,
But turn to ashes in the hand,
    Whose roses, ere they bloom, still die.

But, as the bow her sign sends up
    O'er troubled waves, from suffering spring
The calmer peace, the brighter hope,
    Whose home is where the angels sing.
Is there a pleasure we for pain
    Would not exchange, if so forgiven?
And who their earthly wishes gain,
    Without, perchance, the loss of heaven?

[1] Atlantis.   [2] Shores of the Dead Sea.

III.

THE NUNS' EVENING-HYMN TO THE BLESSED VIRGIN.

"Henceforth all generations shall call me blessed."
Luke i. 48.

MOTHER of peace![1] whene'er the calm,
The twilight hour we see
With dewy blush retire, we raise
Our thoughts and eyes to thee.

---

[1] "Mother of peace," "mercy," etc., in the sense of her being able to obtain them for us by her prayers.

As possibly, to some readers, this and the next two pieces may seem to savor of superstition at least, the author, especially as the subject is one of much interest, will venture here briefly to remark that they greatly err who suppose that the practice of invoking the *intercessory* aid of the saints is confined solely to the Catholic, and Greek and other Oriental Churches. Even Luther himself says (Prep. ad Mort.), "Let no one omit to call upon the Blessed Virgin and the angels and saints, that they may intercede with God for them at the instant" (of dying); and Bishop Montague, considered one of the brightest lights of the Established Church of England, observes (Treat. Invoc. of Saints), "It is no impiety to say, *Holy Mary, pray for me; Holy Peter, pray for me.*" It would seem probable that the Lutheran Churches, at least the stricter of them, still recommend what their founder so earnestly enjoins, and that, in his, the bishop, in regard to his belief on this point, was not likely to have stood alone. That both the doctrine and practice of invoking the prayers of the saints are agreeable to nearly all, if not indeed all, the ancient *fathers* and *doctors* of the Church, is admitted (if their remarks on this topic be collectively taken) by the *Protestant* writers, Fulk (Rejoinder to Bristow, and upon 2 Pet. i.), Thorndike (in Epig. 3), Brightman (in Apoc. 14), and the Centuriators of Magdeburg (cent. 4), all of whom had doubtless consulted their works in the original Greek and Latin. Indeed, this at least *poetically* beautiful and consolatory devotion is, even now, practiced by at least four-fifths of the portion, that calls itself Christian, of the human race. The advocates for it, if weight of authority and numbers are to be regarded, appear to have much the best of the argument.

Mother of mercy! seat of all
Sweet, kind affections, hear!
As now, with humble plea, we kneel,
And penitential tear.

Mother of hope! o'er life's dark sea
Bright and unsetting sign;
Mother of God! to whose prayer will
He list, if not to thine?

Mother of joy! before whose smile
Our troubles flee, as, where
Beams on the night thy emblem bright,[1]
The clouds dissolve to air.

Sad, sinful souls, we hardly dare
To raise our eyes to heaven:
Pray thou for us! oh, pray! and we
May hope to be forgiven.

IV.

ÆGEAN VESPERS.

ORA *pro nobis!*[2] With the dying moan
Of wind and wave, the vesper-hymn we hear,
O'er the calm deep more faintly breathed, and lone,
And tremulous, as uttered with a tear:

---

[1] Crescent moon.
[2] See note to the piece next preceding this.

For now, with oar suspended, glide we near
The convent, fading, mid the twilight pale;
  And pausing, lo! the wayworn mountaineer,
  And passing voyager, with slackened sail,
Thee, Mary, ever blest, sweet Virgin-Mother, hail.

Oh! never may this weary heart forget
  The hour which bids us raise our thoughts to thee!
Those gracious eyes, meek mercy's own, oh! let
  Them ever plead for sad humanity!
Whether, as now, far o'er the lonely sea
The daylight fades, or gilds the forest wild,
  The city dome,—where'er our path may be,
Oh! ever still affectionate and mild,
In pity for us plead, like mother for her child!

v.

THE DEATH OF ST. CLARA.

SHE slept not, and yet seemed to sleep,
  While rose the evening prayer,[1]
And tones more sadly soft and sweet
  Were heard in air.

The angels knew she was to die,
  And soon to be with them,
And so they left their choirs, to sing
  Her requiem.

[1] Sung at vespers.

But once she raised her eye; it met
The holy sign[1] that lay,
Beside the lily, on her breast,
 Then closed for aye.

Softly, like vesper incense, passed
Her soul, at dewy eve,
To where the bright, the chosen few,
 Their crowns receive.

Oh, happy spirit! now like them
From sin and suffering free,
Pray thou for us! we have no cause
 To pray for thee.

VI.

TO THE INFANT SAVIOUR.

A Christmas Hymn

WE know why Thou wert born,
 At midnight, cold, forlorn,
Each brighter star, perchance, obscured or set;
 A little straw Thy bed,
 No pillow for Thy head,
Thy swaddling-clothes Thy only coverlet:—
 It was that we might *love* Thee.

[1] Crucifix.

Hadst—with the glorious band,
    That in Thy presence stand
Waiting Thy will—Thou come, O dearest Lord!
    In gold and purple drest,
    A King, nay God, confest,
Oh! then we had with awe-struck gaze adored,
    But, ah! might not have loved Thee.

    I see the shepherds spread,
    To shield Thy houseless head
From the cold wind, their fleecy cloaks; I hear
    The whispered prayers they make,
    I see them kneeling take
Thy little hand, and from it kiss the tear
    Thou weep'st, that they may love Thee.

    I see Thy Mother's smile,
    Yet hear her sigh, the while
She muses what Thy suffering lot may be;
    I see her o'er Thee bend
    With Joseph, as they tend
Thy wants with pitying care, and silent plea,
    That all the world may love Thee.

    Thy cradle is the hard,
    Cold manger, but Thy guard
Adoring seraphs, who, with folded wing
    Veiling Thy closed eyes, keep
    A still watch o'er Thy sleep:
Oh, would, sweet Babe, my God, my heavenly King!
    That we, like them, could love Thee!

VII.

THE PENANCE OF ST. MARY OF EGYPT.

She is said, after having led an abandoned life in Egypt, to have retired to a solitude beyond the Jordan, and there lived and died a great penitent.

SHE wanders where by Jordan sleep
   The moonbeam pale and willow sere:
There sighs the reed, the lily weeps,
Bedewed with her repentant tear;
Reminding her of days, when she
Was spotless as the vestal flower—
Blest days! alas, how much unlike
Her dark and penitential hour!

Unbound her locks, the braids they wore
Of gems and gold unheeded lie;
For, lo! the cross, where imaged still
Her Lord and Saviour seems to die.
Oh! how can she there fix her eye,
Nor weep for sins, which, though forgiven,
Seem as their memory must remain
And need repentance e'en in heaven!

Where now the brow the myrtle wreathed?
The Lydian air, the Teian lute,
The flattering lips, that still, where breathed
The music of her own, were mute?

The airy step that led the dance?
The cheek the rose-bloom fades beside?
The jewels that, beneath her glance,
Their dazzling lustre seemed to hide?

Like one she seems whose thoughts from earth
No comfort seek, no trouble fear,
But live for God alone, nor ask
From human eye a smile or tear;
Like one who feels, to heaven's gate,
Though still she soars with patient wing,
Some sin she yet must expiate,
Ere fold it where the angels sing.

VIII.

PENITENCE.

A Hymn for Lent.

I SEE Thee, Jesus! on the cross,
And feel Thy every wound;
I see Thy hand the iron pierce,
And hear the hammer sound:
I see the thorns, the blood, the tears
That, with it mingling, fall;
Thy bleeding limbs; and hear the strokes
They bore in Pilate's hall.

Oh! let me ne'er forget what all
These sufferings mean—that they
The ransom for my guilty soul
Alone can ever pay.
'Twas I, dear Saviour! helped to cause
Those cruel wounds: ah! why
Should I not love for Him to weep
Who loved for me to die?

IX.

MATINS.

HER starry watch withdraws the night,
    Her woodland hymn the morning hears,
And earth with heaven seems, dewy, bright,
    To meet with smiles, and yet with tears.

So should thy earlier offering be:
    Let thanks, with joyful praise, precede;
Then bow thy heart as well as knee,
    And, weeping, for forgiveness plead.

Thanks to the Power whose pencil stains
    Yon rosy cloud, yon azure skies,
Some glory yet to earth remains,
    Some relic of her paradise!

Rise! with the birds thy song begin,
  Ere yet the day's bright orb be seen,
Thy song of praise; and mourn for sin,
  As mourned the dying Magdalene.

X.

LIFE BEYOND THE GRAVE.

SAY not the soul must perish here,
  For endless being though she sigh:
Were this her home, her only sphere,
  Oh! who is there would fear to die?
Then look above, nor vainly try
  To make of earth a paradise;
But trust to Faith's unerring eye,
  Whose home is Immortality's.

CIRCE AND TELEMACHUS.

Telemachus, while searching for Ulysses, is supposed to have been wrecked on the island of Circe, who, enamoured of him, would persuade him to resolve not to leave it.

CIRCE.

OH! where be happy if not here?
    Here are but summer hours;
The rainbow, ever in the sky,
See imaged in the flowers;
Cool fountains, groves whose every leaf
Perfumes the breeze they shade;
And birds whose music shames the pipe
Hermes to Argus played.

TELEMACHUS.

Goddess, no home are these gay bowers,
These idle halls, for me;
A hero's son, I would my deeds,
My fame, like his, should be.

No! would yon bark were mine, and I
Once more upon the wave!
Toil is but pastime to the free,
And peril scorn the brave.

CIRCE.

Ah! what's the fame, what but a name,
You, though it ever flies,
Still hope to win by deeds of bold,
Yet haply vain, emprise?—
What but the star that seems to crown
The hill-top it shines o'er,
Yet, as we climb, is found to be
As distant as before?

TELEMACHUS.

Oh! what for me a life like this—
Howe'er we it may name,
Thy immortality though I,
Power, isle, should share—but shame?
Mine be the meed of glorious deed,
The goal by hardship won
And peril, as the eagle soars
Through tempest to the sun!

CIRCE.

Oh, foolish boy! son of a sire
Wrongly reputed wise,

Go! seek him, wretch, if still alive,
The scorn of earth and skies.
The bower, I vainly decked for him,
Again I deck for thee :
No farther roam—be this thy home,
Thy Ithaca, with me.

TELEMACHUS.

Deck not the bower, tune not the lute !
The garland-rose you twine—
The stone my pillow, turf my bed—
Befits no brow like mine.
Crown not the cup, scent not the couch,
The wreath! The soul that still—
And such is mine—the tempter would
Disarm, has but to will.

THE ARTIST'S GRAVE.

AS here, beside thy humble grave,
I stand and mark the spot,
Where wild weeds unmolested wave,
And genius sleeps forgot,
I feel thy low, unhonored place
Of rest thus lone to see—
One eye, at least, a tear, one heart
A sigh has left for thee.

I met thee in thy noon of life
And enviable state
Of fame, a height which few aspired
To reach, or emulate.
Thy pencil bid the ivory seem
To live, and it obeyed,
Appeared to breathe, nay think, impart
A soul to light and shade.

Those days are gone, forever gone,
And here alone I stand,

No more to greet thy friendly smile,
And grasp thy friendly hand;
To feel I ne'er shall meet thy like,
Nor pause to mark the stone
That crowns some haply worthless dust,
Where should have slept thy own.

The pencil from whose touch to life
The tablet seems to spring;
The sympathies that, like the air,
Embrace each living thing;
Soul, music, wit, converse that bids
The hours as moments flee;—
These seem as with thee gone, as they
Were never more to be.

DEFINITIONS.

THE TIME-SERVER.

WITH him the first in right is first in sway,
And conscience only but the hope of pay.

THE PULPIT QUACK.

To zeal inspired, not Greek, he makes pretence,
And never wants he words, if always sense;
The reason is, the first are stolen pelf,
But for the last still trusts he to himself.

THE REVEL.

O N ! Time with flying footstep press,
  Let music breathe and wine-cup flow,
As hours were years, and happiness
  A dweller, not a guest, below;
As revel's night were ne'er to close,
  And sorrow had for cheeks that bloom,
And beaming eyes, that mock repose,
  No tear in store, and earth no tomb.

As yet the dewy day-star sleeps;
  No rest! till woke, as moonlight flies,
On faded cheeks he coldly peeps,
  On weary feet, and watching eyes:
No rest! Enough that day-beams bright
  To hours of care and toil belong;
On! cease not till they wake! the night
  Was made for mirth, for love and song.

So says the wish that rules the hour;
  Till seems—as sound the dance, the lute,

The laugh, in this Circean bower—
  Each better angel gone, or mute:
For hearts that now his whispers shun,
  Perchance await atoning years;
And few the nights, as here begun,
  That end with smiles, if not with tears.

SONG.

I DREAMED I heard, where wild-flowers grew,
  The morning song of bird and bee:
The rose was there—"But where," I said,
"The rose's lover,[1] where is he?"

So, words from many lips I hear
That music seem to all but me;
To other ears they may be sweet,
But not to mine till spoke by thee.

[1] The nightingale.

VISION OF JUNE.

I SEE thee, June! Thy bright, blue eye
And rosy cheek, foretell the hours
Of cloudless skies and leafy shades,
Of singing birds and blowing flowers.
She comes! the summer's bridemaid: air
Seems but one odor, song, to cheer
This first-born heiress of the Spring,
And loveliest handmaid of the year.

Now here she plucks a leafy twine,
Wherewith her brow to shade; now there,
Some half-blown rose, or lily-bud—
A jewel for her lustrous hair;
Nor them alone, but every flower
To which the bee is singing, till
She pauses where, at noon, the flock
Reposes on the breezy hill.

At length the wood-bird to his mate
His evening song has trilled; then, lone,

She sits, where drowsy brooklets chide
Their banks, with dark-eyed violets sown:
Where wild-vine bower and unpruned brake
In dewy, odorous silence sleep,
Till morn, to music as they wake,
Salutes them from the eastern steep.

I hail thee, June! but, as I trace
Thy sylvan haunts, no longer see
The mate who sought thy streams and shades,
The maid who pulled thy rose, with me.
They sleep where thy own garlands strew
Their graves; and, though thy balmy sky,
Thy odorous bloom, and woodland choir
I greet—'tis not without a sigh.

TO A NUN HEARD SINGING.

WHEN to my closing eye this world
And all its bright illusions fade,
And on my heart the dull, cold hand
Of death, to still its throb, is laid,
Oh, lady! let some voice like thine
Breathe, as from heaven's own blissful sphere,
One cheering tone, and I shall deem
My spirit is already there.

TO A PICTURE.

HOW to the living features true,
  The lip, the eye, the cheek!
And yet why bid the ivory seem,
  As here, to all but speak?
We need no picture to recall—
  Whate'er the limner's art—
The lineaments of one who still
  Is imaged to the heart.

LEADERS OF THE AMERICAN REVOLUTION.

THEY waited not for trump or drum,
  To bid them to the conflict press,
But stepped forth from their forest-home,
  Like lions from the wilderness;
Their rights to claim in words that woke
  The coward to a sense of wrong;
If words should fail, to wield the stroke
  Of Freedom's sword, and shout her song.

RELICS OF NOBILITY.

GO! then, to heroes, sages if allied,
    Go! trace the scroll, but not with eye of pride,
Where truth depicts their glories as they shone,
And leaves a blank where should have been your own.

Mark the pure beam on yon dark wave imprest!
So shines the star on that degenerate breast;
Each twinkling orb that burns with borrowed fires!
So ye reflect the glory of your sires.

TO A WHITE LILY.

COMPANION of my solitary hours,
    Vestal of Nature's temple, nun of flowers,
Bending thy graceful form, as if in prayer,
Incensing with thy breath the morning air,
Thou seem'st to bid us kneeling give to Heaven
Our earliest thoughts. Ah! that, to be forgiven,
We had no cause to kneel! then had not I
Beheld thy stainless beauty with a sigh.

WRITTEN IN AN ALBUM.

WHEN the morning flower sends up
Incense from her dewy cup,
    Maiden, pray for me!
When the noontide shadows sleep,
When the stars their vigils keep,
    Maiden, pray for me!

When the vernal rills are gushing,
When the summer rose is blushing,
    Maiden, pray for me!
When the autumn leaves are dying,
When the wintry winds are sighing,
    Maiden, pray for me!

MITYLENE.[1]

HERE Sappho loved, and sang as ne'er
    Sang woman since, and still I seem,
In this Circean air, to hear
The sigh of her impassioned dream.
Oh! when in aught of lyric strain
Shall breathe a soul like hers again!

VERSION OF A GREEK RELIC.[2]

THOU'RT like the apple—maiden, young and fair!—
    That sees its fellows gathered, one by one,
While, where the topmost leaflet scents the air,
It unmolested sits and blooms alone:—
Forgotten? no! a mark for every eye,
But for the gazer's longing hand too high.

[1] Still a considerable city, and the capital of the island of its name, the ancient Lesbos. Its present most interesting feature, however, we found to be "The Port of Olives," expanding from a narrow entrance into a solitary basin several miles in diameter, surrounded by high hills thickly clad to their very summits with olive-trees. The most beautiful of the Greek islands are perhaps this and its neighbor, Scio. The combined influences of their climate, situation, and scenery, would almost seem to necessitate the poetry and music for which they were formerly so remarkable.

[2] In a note to Hist. Lit., Ancient Greece, it is supposed that the author of this beautiful relic may have been Sappho.

EPISTLE TO A BELLE.

In the manner of Swift.

CELIA, your virtues I commend,
But with the caution of a friend;
For compliment to creature human
Is—but especially to woman,
As to the weak are wine and victual,
A drop, a crumb are scarce too little.
But here you'll mind me of my duty,
And bid me not forget your beauty.
Now for a simile: let's see—
I think I have one "to a tee."
Beauty is like a glass before
A picture set, that, if its pore
The features, without speck or fracture,
Transmit of Healy's[1] manufacture,
For tint and outline much commended,
Does all for what it was intended.
Now what the picture to the glass is,
The soul of woman to her face is;

[1] The eminent artist.

Through which, if we the traits but spy
Of heart and head for which we sigh,
No matter though, at first sight, it
Should put us in a fright or fit,
At length, improving by degrees,
Like wine by age, 'tis sure to please:
A truth that, pondered well, I wot
Has cost full many a Jack a thought,
And made, though neither plump nor fair,
His Gill at last seem debonair.

Launched on the world with sense to guide,
But in its ways as yet untried,
You mind me of a bark that, though
The pilot how to shun may know
Bare rock, or whirlpool, yet, if crossed
By hidden shelf or quicksand, 's lost:
For still the Tempter'd make us ween
No mischief's there where none is seen.
Fops will about you buzz and flit,
The bugs, transfix them with your wit!
Wasps, that would rob you of your honey,
I. e., your morals and your money;
At ball and levee you'll be noted,
Your dullest things as *bonmots* quoted;
And that, for which you will *éclat*
Rightly deserve, as a *faux pas*.
So, be not anxious there to shine,
(You know the proverb, "Husks for swine,")

But keep your pearls for those who'll prize,
More than your acres and your eyes,
The rarer gifts, which are to them
As to its setting is the gem.
E'en knave or fool, howe'er he may
Complexion and *per centum* weigh,
Would rather not, I trow, dispense,
In maid or wife, with worth and sense.

But here methinks I hear you say,
"Man! where's your breeding, sure, I pray?
You'll scarce expect one at eighteen
To die of Paley[1] and the spleen.
Each night I'm on my knees by two,
If not too sleepy, or at loo;
My prayers, each morn, at ten I read,
And seldom (if they're short) in bed;
And Doctor D—— to hear I hope
When next he'll preach against the pope.
Sir! you forget; I'd be your debtor
Not for a sermon, but a letter."

[1] Author of "Paley's Moral Philosophy."

SCOTCH EPISTLE TO A FRIEND ON HIS MARRIAGE.

RESPECIT SIR:
                Though ye're my debtor,
It may be for a friendly letter,
Th' occasion's sic, perchance ye may
Expect frae *me* a line or sae.[1]

Nae doubt ye'll think it straunge indeed
I write as if ayont the Tweed;
But 'tis a truth, ye'll shortly con,
That as the wife is, sae the mon.[2]

I kenn'd 'twas for some weighty reason
We miss'd ye here sae late 'n the season,
Somethin ye didna care for spreadin,
Either a funeral, or a weddin;
But now a'[3] apprehension's past,
Nor muckle grieve I 'twas the last.
It also gies me na sma' pleasure
To learn, in this same nuptial measure,

---

[1] So.   [2] The bride of the writer was of Scotland.   [3] All.

That leads sae mony, when too late,
To curse, if not themsel, their fate,
Ye'll never hae excuse to rue
What half monkind sae sadly do,
When Love awa' his bow maun fling
And mak a halter of the string:
In ither words, possest of ane
Sae fairly spotless of a' stain,
(If that be true o' which I'm hearin,)
'Tis your ain faut if things gae jarrin.

That ilka comin joy be thine
Is not your ain wish mair than mine
Or hers, who soon, it is my prayer,
May hae your likeness in an heir;
For, faith! the warld is bad indeed,
And needs some ane to mend the breed.

I am still, as becomes me duly,
Respecit sir, yours vera truly.

www.ingramcontent.com/pod-product-compliance
Lightning Source LLC
Chambersburg PA
CBHW031450160426
43195CB00010BB/925